# Active Shooter Awareness and Response

*www. ravenadvsry.com*

# Active Shooter Awareness and Response

*Paul D. LeFavor*

**Blacksmith Publishing**

Fayetteville, North Carolina

*Prevention is the best cure.*

Active Shooter Awareness and Response
by Paul D. LeFavor

Copyright © 2021 by Blacksmith LLC

ISBN 978-1-7329681-7-2

Printed in the United States of America

Published by Blacksmith LLC
Fayetteville, North Carolina

www.BlacksmithPublishing.com

Direct inquiries and/or orders to the above web address.

All rights reserved. Except for use in review, no portion of this book may be reproduced in any form without the express written permission from the publisher.

This book does not contain classified or sensitive information restricted from public release. The views presented in this publication are those of the author and do not necessarily represent the Department of Homeland Security or its components.

While every precaution has been taken to ensure the reliability and accuracy of all data and contents, neither the author nor the publisher assumes any responsibility for the use or misuse of information contained in this book.

## Contents

Foreword .................................................................. xi

Prologue ................................................................. xii

Introduction .............................................................. 1

**Chapter**

1 – Staying in the Yellow ............................................. 7

2 – The Usual Suspects ............................................. 24

3 – Decisive Action: Detect – Deny – Defend ............... 39

4 – Awareness and Response in Businesses .................. 53

5 – Awareness and Response at Schools ...................... 65

6 – Awareness and Response at Places of Worship ....... 79

7 – Self-Defense ...................................................... 94

8 – Stop the Bleeding ............................................. 100

9 – Arrival of Law Enforcement & Medical Services ..... 118

10 – Post Incident ................................................. 123

11 – Comprehensive Security PLAN ........................... 133

12 – Conclusion .................................................... 139

About the Author ................................................. 151

Annex A: Fundamentals of Marksmanship ................. 153

Index: ................................................................. 161

Other Books by Blacksmith Publishing ...................... 163

## *List of Mass Shootings*

| | |
|---|---|
| Atlanta Day Trade | 62 |
| Aurora Cinema 16 | 59 |
| Columbine High School | 30 |
| Emmanuel AME | 90 |
| Gabrielle Giffords | 63 |
| Luby's Cafeteria | 59 |
| New Life Church | 86 |
| Pulse Nightclub | 53 |
| Route 91 Harvest Music Festival | 90 |
| Sandy Hook Elementary School | 69 |
| Santa Fe High School | 137 |
| San Ysidro McDonalds | 58 |
| Stoneman Douglas High School | 71 |
| Sutherland Springs First Baptist Church | 80 |
| Thurston High School | 76 |
| Tree of Life Synagogue | 77 |
| Trolley Square Mall | 60 |
| UNC Charlotte | 149 |
| Virginia Tech | 65 |
| West Freeway Church of Christ | 94 |

*Dedicated to those who have fallen in this fight against evil.*

# *Foreword*

"The rifle itself has no moral stature, since it has no will of its own. Naturally, it may be used by evil men for evil purposes, but there are more good men than evil, and while the latter cannot be persuaded to the path of righteousness by propaganda, they can certainly be corrected by good men with rifles." – Jeff Cooper

"A well-regulated militia, being necessary to the security of a free State, the right of the people to keep and bear arms shall not be infringed." These words, adopted in the Constitution of the United States on December 15, 1791, are not to blame for the senseless taking of life by cowards with guns. Mass shootings understandably create public horror and outrage. Since the 1966 mass shooting at University of Texas, there have been 160 mass shootings which together have claimed the lives of over 1,000 innocent people.

As this book will argue, the active shooter phenomenon is a highly complex problem that evades a simple solution. While we wait for a solution, this book offers a conceptual framework to do all that is possible to prevent an attack and the mental tools necessary to defend yourself and others against a threat when there is no other option. The incentive to read this book is, it may save your life.

Sheffield Ford III<br>
CEO, Raven Advisory LLC

## *Prologue*

*"When you attain the Way of strategy there will not be one thing you cannot see. You must study hard."*
– Miyamoto Musashi

Awareness is the key to defeating any threat. Active Shooters are like a can without a label. You never know what's inside until you open it. Some will turn their weapon on themselves when law enforcement arrives and more and more, we are seeing they will stand and fight with law enforcement. They all have different motivations and different methodologies of attack. A knife, a handgun, a rifle, an explosive, a vehicle, etc. Active Shooters are only limited by their imagination. Your response is only limited by your imagination. The reality is that the killing will often be done by the time law enforcement arrives. It is YOU that will decide the outcome if you are amid an Active Shooter.

Your survival depends on a strategy and that strategy requires awareness through education and understanding your environment, your options, and developing a successful strategy to defeat any threat. Responding to an Active Shooter takes 3 key approaches. Just like the car service AAA that can tow you out of anything these 3 A's will tow you out of an Active Shooter Incident and give you a path to survival. Attitude, Awareness, and Action. The ATTITUDE that you are not preparing for the probability but rather the possibility, the

AWARENESS of any environment you are in routes of egress, safe-havens, and field expedient weapons, and last but not least ACTION if you have to fight have a plan and fight hard because hesitation kills in an Active Shooter Incident.

The book Active Shooter Awareness and Response by Paul D. Lefavor is a must-read for all citizens. Our daily news is filled with weekly occurrences of Active Shooter incidents. Whether you are working in business, attending or teaching at a school, or attending a service at your local house of worship the author enhances your situational awareness and puts some tools in your toolbox to survive. The author successfully takes you down the path of awareness, the threats, strategy, environments of encounters, defense, first aid, first responder encounters, and post-incident actions. All of the above subjects are constantly reinforced via real-life examples to drive the teaching points home. The author gives you slides in your subconscious through graphic details of actual incidents to draw upon if you are ever exposed to an Active Shooter.

John "Randy" Butler<br>
President/CEO<br>
Law Enforcement Associates Response Network<br>
(LEARN International) LLC<br>
Full Mission Profile (FMP) LLC

# Introduction

*"A problem well defined, explored and clarified is well on its way to be managed."*

Mass shootings scare the hell out of us. This is due partly because of their seemingly random nature and our inability to predict or often prevent them from happening and taking the lives of those we hold dear.

Over the past decade there have been a number of high-profile, active shooter events which have occurred around the world. An *active shooter* is an armed person(s) who uses any type of weapon to inflict serious harm and/or deadly physical force on others in public and continues to do so while having access to additional victims. Examples of active shooter attacks include an active shooter incident, mass stabbings, explosives, vehicle-as-a-weapon, fire-as-a-weapon, and so forth.[1] There is a degree of ambiguity when it comes to the definitions "active shooter" and "mass shooting." In this book, the term mass shooting will be used to describe active shooter incidents.

In light of such tragic events as the attacks at Columbine High School (1999), Virginia Tech (2007), Fort Hood (2009), etc., a concerted effort has been

---

[1] White Paper for the Integrated Public Safety Response to the Active Shooter/Active Shooter available from https: file:///G:/3.%20Blacksmith%20Publishing/2%20-%20Sword/2%20-%20Shooter%20Awareness%20and%20Response/State-of-North-Carolina-Active-Shooter-White%20Paper-02Aug2017.pdf accessed 27 December 2018.

made to be better prepared to address the active shooter threat. Crucial to your ability to survive a violent threat is an ability to maintain situational awareness, detect a threat and defend yourself and others.

A 2019 report by the FBI, "A Study of Active Shooter Incidents in the United States Between 2000 and 2018," provides an updated look at the statistics. The bureau defines an "active shooter" as "one or more individuals actively engaged in killing or attempting to kill people in a populated area." The FBI found that during the period studied, 277 active-shooter incidents took place in the United States, resulting in 884 killed and 1,546 wounded — 2,430 casualties in all.

Of the 277 surveyed events, 160 involved a single shooter. Except for six events, men conducted the vast majority of attacks. Most incidents were rapid: 60% ended before police arrived, 44 (69%) of 64 incidents ended in five minutes or less, with 23 ending in two minutes or less. In 21 (13.1%) of 160 incidents, unarmed individuals attempted to neutralize active shooters. In 11 of those, unarmed principals, teachers, other school staff and students confronted the shooters to end the threat. In almost 30% of the cases, law enforcement agents and the shooter exchanged fire. In 45 of the 160 incidents where agents engaged a shooter, they suffered casualties in 21 (46.7%) of the

## Introduction

incidents, resulting in nine officers killed and 28 wounded.

In line with previous findings, the report found that the attacks were generally perpetrated in commercial areas (73 out of 160 or 45.6%). In 24 of the 160 shooting incidents (15%) more than one location was involved. Schools were the second-largest grouping (39 out of 160, or 24.4%), and 10% took place in government properties. The majority of the incidents (90 out of 160, or 56.3%) ended when the shooter committed suicide, surrendered or fled the scene. Of these, the shooter committed suicide at the scene after law enforcement arrived but before officers could act. It is the pressure of law enforcement arriving that leads to the shooter committing suicide; the shooter is no longer in control of the situation. To borrow from Mark Warren "this is when the victimizer returns to being the victim."

An Active Shooter is an individual actively engaged in killing or attempting to kill people in a confined and populated area. There is no pattern or method to their selection of victims. Active shooter situations are unpredictable and evolve quickly. Typically, the immediate deployment of law enforcement is required to stop the shooting and mitigate harm to victims. Because active shooter situations are often over within 10 to 15 minutes, before law enforcement arrives on the scene, individuals must be prepared both mentally and physically to deal with an active shooter situation.

Active shooter attacks are dynamic incidents that vary greatly from one attack to another. Given the suddenness of most active shooting incidents, our goal is to be armed with a conceptual framework for which we may observe the environment, read the human terrain and be mentally prepared to defend ourselves and others against an attack and take lethal action if necessary.

The purpose of this book is to provide you, the law abiding American, with a better awareness of the active shooter phenomenon so as to detect a threat and develop a subconscious response that will put you on the best footing to deny the threat's ability to kill you and those around you, defending yourself with proportionate force.

To that end, this book will discuss techniques to profile a threat, our decision cycle once the threat is underway, and several tactics one can use to defend ourselves against an active shooter. An effort will also be made to highlight various societal factors that contribute to this phenomenon. Perception is based on one's worldview. Particularly, many believe that guns are the problem. And that, removing all guns from society would be the panacea. This book will argue that that position is neither tenable nor realistic, nor constitutional. As another strand to this argument, citing incomplete facts, many believe these

## Introduction

senseless slaughters are perpetrated by the mentally ill. As will be argued, this too is an argument based on assumptions and incomplete facts.

While acknowledging these issues, as will be argued, the active shooter phenomenon is in fact a complex socially conditioned disaster consisting of various elements which is, in the last analysis, a media-stimulated sensation.

The impetus of this book was to systematize the various methodologies being offered to the public to be the best prepared against the active shooter phenomenon. These methodologies include the Department of Homeland Security's "Run/Hide/Fight," "Avoid, Deny, Defend" which was developed by the Texas State University, and "ALICE: Alert, Lockdown, Inform, Counter, Evacuate" developed by Navigate 360.

With that in mind, this book is divided into twelve chapters. In chapters one and two, our purpose is to lay a foundation for the conceptual skills of having situational awareness, including threat profiling. Building on this, chapter three introduces the decisive action methodology of detect – deny – defend with the aim of developing an ability to rapidly assess a situation and decisively make a critical decision. Chapters four to six seeks to provide preventative and defensive tactics for the mitigation of active shooter situations at schools, places of worship and businesses.

*Active Shooter Awareness and Response*

 Chapter seven deals with self-defense, chapter eight is a guide to casualty care. Chapter nine will inform us of what to do as law enforcement and emergency medical teams arrive. Then, chapters ten and eleven will focus on post-incident activities and a strategy to build a comprehensive security plan. Finally, chapter twelve will tie things together in an effort for us to put our best foot forward toward this threat. Overall, the argument presented will be prevention is the best cure.

 In preparing this book, I am grateful to several people for their help. I would like to thank Mike Blackburn, Sheffield Ford, David Heldt, Billy Varga, Chris Hicks, Reagan Bownds, Randy Butler, Byron Low, Terry Buchanan, and Robert Owen. Thanks to all.

Paul D. LeFavor<br>
Camp Mackall, NC<br>
Spring 2021

# 1

## *Staying in the Yellow*

*"Life works because things have a "normal." But, when something is off, out of place, or unusual, we know that something isn't right. Unfortunately, most people don't do anything when "something isn't right." They don't allow their intuition to guide them. They don't proactively seek to determine what is out of place, they don't step back to observe the situation more closely, or they don't duck. It is only after the situation has occurred—in hindsight—when they realize something was out of place."* – Left of Bang

There's a scene at the beginning of *The Bourne Identity* where the film's protagonist Jason Bourne is sitting in a diner, trying to figure out who he is and why he has a bunch of passports and a gun stashed in a safe deposit box. Bourne also notices things that other people don't. In fact, it seems as though he has a superhuman ability to observe his surroundings and make detailed assessments about his environment. His ability to rapidly assess his surroundings would greatly aid his survivability in a crisis. However, this is not just a trait possessed by top secret operatives. It's a skill known as situational awareness, a mindset that is learned over time through repetition and muscle memory and you can possess it too.

The term situational awareness (SA) is a concept that serves as a label for a range of cognitive activities. Simply put, SA is knowing what is going on around you. SA is defined as the perception of environmental elements and events with respect to time or space, the comprehension of their meaning, and the projection of their status in the near future.[1] In other words, SA is being aware of your surroundings and is key to a great many things, including surviving an active shooter incident.

As argued by Mica Endsley, traditional wisdom provides us with three elements or levels of SA: perception, comprehension, and projection. Perception is our sense of the situation principally through sight and sound. Comprehension integrates multiple pieces of information to determine their relevance, and projection enables us to forecast future events based on the factors at hand. In other words, SA means having a clear picture of what is happening, how it got that way, and how it might further develop.

Underscoring the importance of SA, in most after-action reports of shootings, survivors bear witness to people or events that were out of place. For instance, before the mass shooting occurred at Virginia Tech, students saw the shooter walk around poking his head into a few classrooms.

An eye witness noted, "it was strange that someone at this point in the semester would be lost, looking for a class." As the Columbine shooting was underway, everyone thought at first it was some sort of prank. The sounds of gunfire were dismissed as firecrackers

---

[1] Mica R. Endsley and Daniel J. Garland, *Situation Awareness Analysis and Measurement* (New York: CRC, 2000), 5.

## Chapter One: Staying in the Yellow

or some other noise. In many cases, there was simply a failure to process and act upon the available information.

Our goal is to not only survive an attack but blunt it. Crucial to this is SA which requires being proactive and continuously alertness. Most people are clueless to their surroundings, often spending much of their time with their faces buried in a cellphone. In order to not become a statistic, you must have SA, you must be able to read both the environment and the people around you. To have SA is to gain a mindset of proactiveness – an ability to sense indicators of an imminent attack, and if possible, thwart it. We want to take on the offensive mindset of a hunter instead of the defensive mindset of prey.

The point is, mental preparation is the foundation for a successful outcome in any conflict. The brain is the first and most influential weapon that we can employ into any dangerous encounter. When you're prepared and aware, you will think your way out of a thousand more situations than you will ever fight your way out of. It is for this reason that situational awareness is more of a mindset than a skill.

One of the goals of this book is to outline a system by which individuals and teams can be the most prepared to defend themselves against senseless attacks. The first aspect of this system is the ABCs of situational awareness. These are:

## Active Shooter Awareness and Response

A – Alert Mindset
B – Behavior Profiling
C – Comprehension and Projection

### *Alert Mindset*

As empirical evidence shows, most mass shootings are over in less than five minutes. On August 4, 2019, 24-year-old Connor Betts shot and killed 9 people and injured 17 others in less than 30 seconds (Ned Peppers Bar, Dayton, Ohio). An aggregate of eye witness accounts strongly suggests that the first five seconds are the most crucial. Having an alert mindset is therefore paramount to putting our best foot forward toward surviving a deadly encounter. Arguably, having an alert mindset begins with knowing where you are. As will be argued, an "Alert Mindset" is MADE by having a **M**ental map, **A**ttentiveness, recognizing a **D**efensive position(s), and having an **E**xit strategy. These steps are not necessarily in order.

**Mental Map** – As said, perception is our sense of the situation we are in, including where we are in reference to other places we know. A mental map is formed in our minds as we realize we are seated in a particular part of a restaurant that is a three second sprint away from the bathrooms and perhaps four from an emergency exit. You should have an idea of where the nearest exit is, and how many exits there

## Chapter One: Staying in the Yellow

are. Mental mapping also seeks to find multiple exits, hardened portions of the building, etc.

**Attentiveness** – Notwithstanding this mental map of where we are, SA starts with being alert. The best way to maintain SA is to stay alert, which may make the difference between life and death. In his seminal book, *Principles of Personal Defense*, retired Marine Lieutenant Colonel Jeff Cooper laid out a color code system to help warriors gauge their mindset for combat scenarios. Each color represents a person's potential state of awareness and focus. Cooper broke down SA into four levels of escalating degrees of preparation: Conditions White, Yellow, Orange, and Red (See figure 1-1).

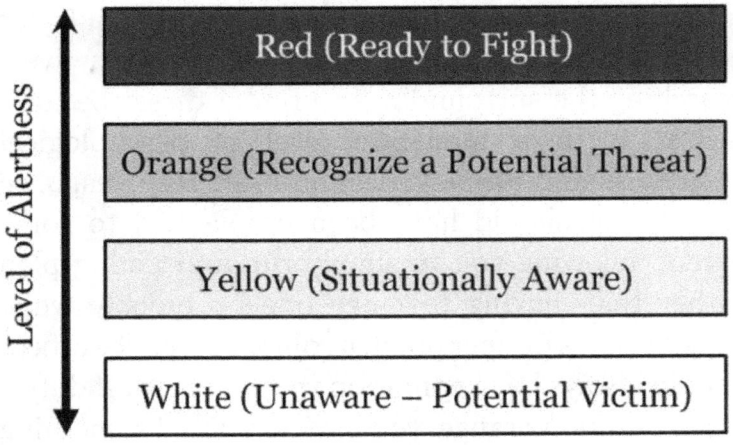

Figure 1-1. Levels of Alertness.

In condition white, you are relaxed and unaware of what is going on around you. In this condition, you are "unprepared and unready to take lethal action." Ideally, you are in white when asleep, but realistically we often drop our guard when we are at home or in some other environment that we assume to be safe. If you are attacked in condition white, statistically speaking you risk a higher chance of death.

In condition yellow, you remain relaxed, but are aware of who and what is around you. This means you are paying attention to the sights and sounds that surround you whether you are at home or moving in society. This is not equated with paranoia or irrational fear. Instead, you simply have moved your alertness to a level of attention that will prevent you from being totally surprised by the actions of another person.

If you are attacked in condition yellow, it should not come as a total surprise. In yellow, we are actively searching the surroundings to find a threat because yellow is in a moderate level of psychological awareness and physiological arousal. Your response to a threat should have been preplanned to some extent, allowing you to simply run an existing plan rather than having to make one up quickly while under fire. As Cooper put it, a competent police officer should always be in condition yellow, on or off duty.

In condition orange, you have identified something that has piqued your interest that may or may not prove to be a threat. Until you determine the true nature of whatever has piqued your interest, your

## Chapter One: Staying in the Yellow

"radar" is narrowed to concentrate on the possible threat and will remain so until you are satisfied that no threat exists. If someone or something looks out of place, you change from a 360-degree SA to a more focused concentration in a specific direction. At the same time, you can't drop your SA, because a threat in front of you may be a distraction for one behind you.

If you are attacked in condition orange, you should be expecting the attack. Further, you will hopefully be facing your attacker since you have already shifted your focus in his direction. If you are well trained, your subconscious mind will have been searching your hard drive for similar events or training sessions you have already experienced (Boyd's "orient" step), as well as any pre-visualized "what if" situations you've cataloged as possible solutions should an attack take place.

If the focus of your attention in condition orange does something you find threatening, you will shift to condition red. Notice here that condition red is not the firing stroke, as some have misconstrued, instead, condition red simply changes the focus of your attention from a potential threat to a potential target. You will draw your weapon, or move still further to sight acquisition, only if the potential target's actions dictate such a response. Once you've shifted to condition red, you cannot be surprised by your primary adversary. But your intense concentration on a forward threat will lessen your ability to maintain some degree of 360-degree SA for unknown threats that may come from other directions. Effective training under high-stress conditions will help you avoid the tunnel vision that some describe as "akin to looking through a toilet paper tube."

If possible, in both conditions orange and red, move to a position that provides a positional advantage. Ideally, you want a wall or previously cleared area behind you and some sort of solid cover you can move behind should shooting break out. If you are attacked in red, you should be fully prepared to defend yourself. Whether or not you have a gun in hand or on target will depend on the circumstances, but mentally, you are already ahead of the game. Cooper's Color Code is important as it allows us to quantify our state of mind and gives us a target of awareness to aim for – condition yellow.

**Defensive Position** – This leads us to consider another aspect of maintaining SA: Having a plan that includes running to a defensive position. Even those who are best prepared will undoubtedly find themselves caught off-guard. This may entail choosing a seat in a restaurant, if possible, to position yourself to see the entrance or to minimize the number of people who might be behind you. You don't need to insist on securing the "gunslinger seat," which will put your back to a dead corner and your face to the entrance, because you are not anticipating a threat, you are merely conducting an inventory of your surroundings and the other people around you. You will also be running a cursory "what if" mental visualization of where a threat could appear and what your reaction might be.

**Exit Strategy** – Putting this all together, we should have an exit strategy. Having a mental map of the building we're in, how long it would take to move those with us to the nearest exit, and where we're parked is a good place to start. Thinking defensively might lead us to consider the nearest weapon of some sort we might use in a pinch. For example, in a restaurant setting, assuming we are not armed, we could use a fire extinguisher (normally located in restaurant kitchens), or even the knife on our table.

Situational Awareness is crucial to not becoming a statistic. It places us in the best mental state to observe our environment for pre-attack indicators. However, we must be able to separate important from unimportant information, for not everything we see is relevant for identifying threats.[2] This leads us to consider the reciprocal aspect of situational awareness – reading the human terrain.

---

[2] Patrick Van Horne and Jason A. Riley, *Left of Bang* (New York: Black Irish Entertainment, 2014), 24.

## ***Behavior-Profiling***

Being more observant is not enough to have good SA, you have to know what you're looking for. This second component, the "B" of the ABCs of SA is behavior-profiling. This aspect of SA incorporates two basic components: establishing baselines and identifying anomalies. A baseline is what is considered normal for any given setting, and includes people, situations and environments. An anomaly is any deviation from the baseline.[3]

For example, when a VIP, such as a public official, walks into a room, we expect individuals to stand and greet them. A variation from this is someone not standing or not greeting them, is an anomaly. Anomalies indicate something has changed in the situation. Often, they are indicators that something is wrong. Another way to classify an anomaly is based on the presence or absence of something. When something (or someone) is not present when it should be, or is present when it shouldn't be, this is an anomaly.

To illustrate further, the baseline at a coffee shop will usually entail people reading a book or working on their computer or speaking in hushed tones with their friends. The baseline at a rock concert would be loud music and people looking at the stage while

---

[3] Ibid., 52.

## Chapter One: Staying in the Yellow

either jumping up and down to the music or swaying their bodies to the beat.

It is also important to note that it's normal for baselines to vary to some degree. Nonetheless, anomalies are indicators of potential threats because they signal changes in situations. Granted, not every change in a situation is bad, but any change in a situation needs to be considered with suspicion. The phrase "something wasn't right" is common lingo among people who have observed anomalies. Police officers use it to describe suspicious behavior, which they might discover was indicative of a crime taking place or a perpetrator.

Just as a hunter observes the ground for signs, an SA skillset that will increase our survivability is behavior-profiling. This involves taking cues from human behavior such as gestures, facial expressions, etc. Because human behavior is predictable, their behavior can predict their actions. For instance, a boxer can pick up on the way their opponent may telegraph moves. Picking up on the behavioral cue can help us predict a move.

There are six domains that capture the most significant aspects of human behavior in simple terms. Knowing these nonverbal forms of communication will help us in situations to establish baselines and identify anomalies. These domains are: Proxemics, geographics, biometrics, kinesics, heuristics and atmospherics. Important to note, behavior profiling does not pertain to racial, gender, age, or religious biases. This acrostic will help you remember them: "**P**resident **G**eorge **B**ush **k**nows **h**is **a**tmospherics."

***Proxemics*** involves reading the relative spatial distances between individuals as a means of evaluating their supposed relationship and intentions. The term "proxemics" was first coined by anthropologist Edward C. Hall in 1963 and involves understanding a person's behavior as it relates to those around them. Proxemic behaviors express attitudes and motivations (See figure 1-2).

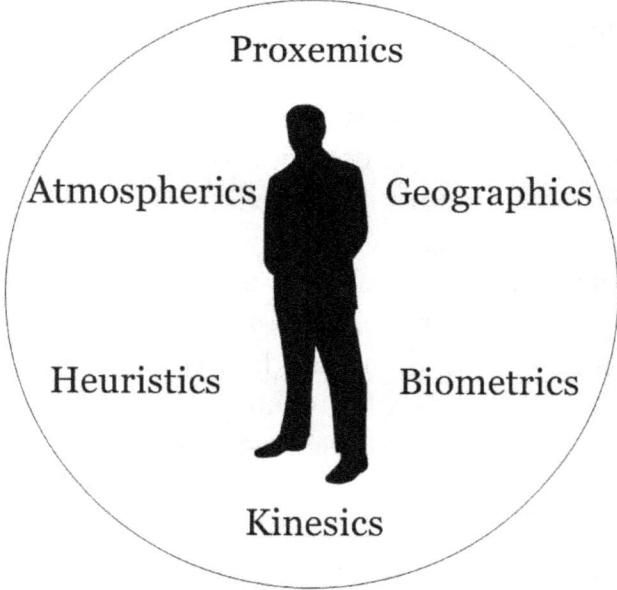

Figure 1-2. Six Domains of Behavior Profiling.

## Chapter One: Staying in the Yellow

Citing an example from the Iraq War, a crowd would often exhibit a proxemic push and keep an unusual distance from an insurgent who was about to carry out an attack on coalition forces. In the above example, the proxemic push expressed a preattack indicator.

**Geographics** involves reading the relationship between people and their environment. Geographics help us pick out who is familiar or unfamiliar with the area they are in. Eye witness accounts of shootings give numerous examples of how the shooter looked "out of place." For example, sounds of gunfire were often dismissed as firecrackers. At Virginia Tech, before the shooting in classrooms began, the perpetrator walked around in the hallway, poking his head into a few classrooms.

**Biometrics** are observable biological reactions that correspond to physiological and/or mental states. Biometrics involves uncontrollable and automatic biological responses to stress. These physiological responses are key to understanding a person's emotional states and changes. For example, a preattack indicator could be a person's discernable fight response. Some obvious biometrics cues could include visible anger, shaking, sweaty palms, being fidgety, etc.

As another example, one of the ways law enforcement was able to identify the Boston Marathon bombers was that they noticed in surveillance footage that the men looked relatively calm while everyone else was running around in a panic. The reason they looked calm was because they knew the explosion was going to happen and thus weren't surprised by it, while everyone else was caught off guard.

**Kinesics** involves how people communicate consciously and subconsciously through posture, gesture, stance and movement.[4] In other words, body language can communicate emotions and possibly future intentions. Picking up on these signals may enable one to proactively identify threats.

For example, law enforcement officers are trained to observe the hands of a person they're interacting with. Hands often telegraph hidden nefarious intentions. People who are concealing something they don't want discovered, like a gun, knife, or stolen object, will often touch or pat that area on the body where that object is concealed, as if to ensure the object has not been lost or is still hidden from view. Regarding posture, those up to no good will try to "act natural." But it's difficult to act natural when you're

---

[4] R. L. Birdwhistell, *Introduction to Kinesics: An Annotation System for Analysis of Body Motion and Gesture* (Washington, DC: Department of State, Foreign Service Institute), 1952.

## Chapter One: Staying in the Yellow

not completely focused on what you are doing. People trying to "act natural" will appear distracted and will over or under exaggerate their movements. These people appear to be trying too hard.

**Heuristics** refers to a process of interpreting observations by matching them to mental models developed through experience, education, or shared knowledge. As argued by Wray Herbert, they are "cognitive rules of thumb."[5] In other words, heuristics makes use of things already known to develop a tactical shortcut that elicits just enough information to draw a reasonable conclusion. Heuristics deal with probability. The easier it is for us to think of a certain type of event happening, the higher we rate its probability.

**Atmospherics** focuses on the collective attitudes, moods, and behaviors in a given situation or a place. In other words, it involves "reading the room" to pick up on social or emotional cues and shifts in the atmosphere that often signal that something significant has changed or that something is about to occur. For example, before an Iraqi reporter threw both his shoes at George W. Bush, the president quickly realized the sudden change in atmospherics. As the shoes hurled his direction, he ducked. Then, as

---

[5] Wray Herbert, *On Second Thought: Outsmarting Your Mind's Hard-Wired Habits* (New York: Crown, 2011), 3.

the reporter was wrestled to the ground Bush said, "if you want to know the facts, it was a size 10." Understanding the collective atmosphere will key you in to attitudes, emotions, and behavior that doesn't fit the given situation—anomalies.

### *Comprehension-Projection*

The third component of SA is comprehension-projection which puts our situation into context so we know what to do with the information. In chapter three, we will introduce the decision cycle (OODA loop). In this step of SA, we want to take what we have gathered and **F**orecast events, **A**nticipate actions (yours and others), and be **R**eady to take action (FAR).

Putting things together looks like this: Every environment and person have a baseline. A baseline is what's "normal" in a given situation, and it will differ from person to person and environment to environment. We establish baselines so that we can spot anomalies. How do we do this? By asking ourselves good questions. Baseline questions: When we enter a new environment or walk into a new building such questions might include: What is considered normal here? What's the general mood of the place? How do most people behave here most of the time? Anomaly questions: What would cause someone or something to stand out? For example, if someone is wearing a jacket in the summer, does that

## Chapter One: Staying in the Yellow

type of clothing fit? What would that indicate? Comprehension-projection questions: Where is all of this going? What do I need to do about what is going on?

### *Summary*

In the analogy of Patrick Van Horne and Jason Patrick A. Riley, the goal is to be "Left of Bang." Bang is the attack. Being left of it requires informed awareness. Many have said the most important principle of war is surprise. Our goal is to not be surprised but to proactively identify threats based on our active assessment of our environment, body language and nonverbal signals. This state of awareness will put us in the best position to detect a threat and then rapidly take action. As has been said, being more observant is not enough. You have to know what you're looking for, and then put that information into context so it has meaning and becomes "actionable."

In light of the casualties that have fallen, it stands to reason that developing a keener sense of SA should be at the top of everyone's list. When we're out, we need to stay in the yellow.

# 2

## *The Usual Suspects*

*"Sometime in April, me and V will get revenge and will kick natural selection up a few notches. If we have figured out the art of time bombs beforehand, we will set hundreds of them around houses, roads, bridges and gas stations, anything that will cause damage and chaos. It'll be like the LA riots, the Oklahoma bombing, WWII, Vietnam, Duke Nukem and Doom all mixed together. I want to leave a lasting impression on the world."* – Eric Harris

As argued by James Knoll and George Annas, the phenomenon of active shooter can be defined as a heavily armed individual who meticulously plans a public massacre in which they intend to spread as much destruction as possible and then kill themselves. Data recently released by the FBI illustrate the annual number of active shooter incidents, which is up sharply since the 2014 (See figure 2-1).

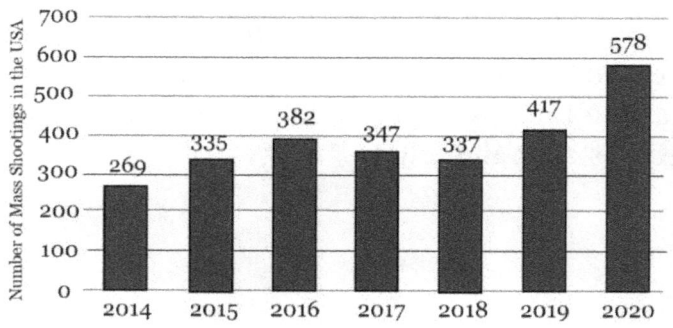

Figure 2-1. Active Shooter Incidents 2014-2018. Source FBI.

## Chapter Two: The Usual Suspects

In 2000, there was only one such incident listed in the FBI's database. Last year, there were 27. That rate works out to about one active shooting incident every 18 days. In other words, the number of people killed or injured annually in active shooter incidents has increased by more than 100%.

*Targeted Locations* – The largest proportion of active shooter incidents (nearly 44%) occurs in areas of commerce, including businesses both open and closed to the public. Generally, 20% of active shooter incidents occur at schools, including colleges and universities; and 13% occur in open spaces, including public streets, open parking lots, and parks. The remaining 23% occurs on government property, residences, health care facilities and houses of worship (See figure 2-2).

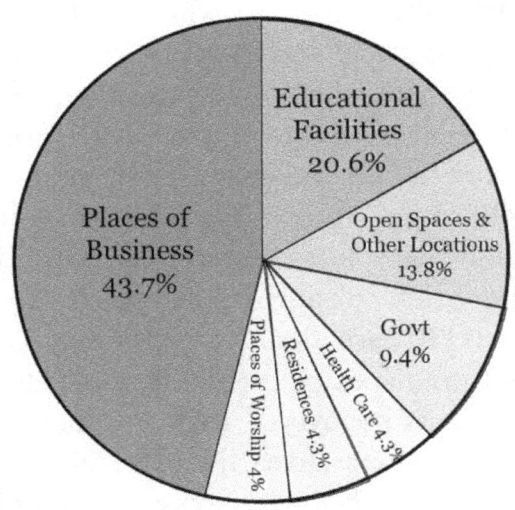

Figure 2-2. Active Shooter Locations. Source FBI.

What kind of person commits mass murder? While the phenomenon of the active shooter has eluded classification and a precise profile remains somewhat speculative, there is a basic demographic similarity. As is generally known, most are white, 20–50-year-old males. Beyond this, however, there has been much speculation that may or may not be intrinsically correct. For example, Madfis (2014) suggests that "rampage shooters" seek power and dominance which they believe is being denied to them. This line of reasoning wrongly suggests that mass shooters, being White, male and middle class, are angered by their being cheated out of their supposed rightful place of social dominance. As will be demonstrated, this discredited interpretation falls short of empirical evidence.

Regarding active shooters, what may be safely said, in the simplest terms, such persons are categorized by mental state and motive. Regarding mental state, scholarly consensus maintains there are several predisposing factors associated with mass shooters. As I will argue, these may be categorized as depression, pathological narcissism and social isolation. A brief look at these will prove useful.

In a 2000 FBI assessment, depression was found to be a major predisposing mental factor. Echoing this, a team analysis uncovered that of adolescent mass shooters, one in four had earlier psychiatric treatment and half of all adult mass shooters had a history of

## Chapter Two: The Usual Suspects

psychiatric treatment. Of these, the primary diagnosis was depression.[1] A 2002 Secret Service survey determined that nearly 80% of school shooters had entertained thoughts of suicide or prior attempts at suicide.[2] Likewise, a 2015 study found that of 185 mass shooters, nearly half committed suicide after the crime.[3]

Another recurring trait that is comorbid with depression is pathological narcissism. According to J. Reid Meloy, in this mental state, a person has delusions of grandeur, demanding they receive the attention they deserve. Pointedly, Meloy argues, in such persons who perpetrate mass shootings, suicide actually satisfies a narcissistic need for attention.[4] He goes on to observe, the "suicidal" communication beforehand may be one aspect of "final act" behavior. This may adequately explain the paradox of those who have delusions of grandeur but are simultaneously so demoralized that their suicidal

---

[1] Meloy, J. Reid, Anthony G. Hempel, B. Thomas Gray, Kris Mohandie, Andrew Shiva, and Thomas C. Richards. "A comparative analysis of North American adolescent and adult mass murderers." *Behavioral Sciences & the Law* 22, no. 3 (2004): 291-309.

[2] Vossekuil, Bryan, Robert A. Fein, Marisa Reddy, Randy Borum, and William Modzeleski. "The final report and findings of the Safe School Initiative." *Washington, DC: US Secret Service and Department of Education* (2002).

[3] Lankford, Adam. "Mass shooters in the USA, 1966–2010: Differences between attackers who live and die." *Justice Quarterly* 32, no. 2 (2015): 360-379.

[4] J. Reid Meloy, "Approaching and attacking public figures: A contemporary analysis of communications and behavior." *Journal of Threat Assessment and Management* 1, no. 4 (2014): 243.

ideation is perceived as "martyrdom." In fact, as Leonard Bobadilla poignantly observes, "their suicidal ideation is channeled as 'martyrdom' against real or perceived opponents," and "those who hate themselves and others so intensely as to seek mutual destruction."[5]

A third cord in this unfortunate triad is social isolation. This predisposing factor is particularly noticeable in school shooters. Generally, it is understood that some 70% of adolescent mass shooters have been characterized as loners, that in many instances were victimized or bullied. In a 2008 analysis, Deborah Weisbrot determined higher levels of threat present in those bullied or socially lone.[6] A survey of history confirms social isolation as a major contributing factor. Being paranoid and socially isolated, in many cases, mass shooters have tended to identify themselves as victims of injustice and their situations as "them versus the world." Having this tendency leads to a rationalization for their crimes.

When these three factors of depression, pathological narcissism and social isolation coalesce, and its tempered with suicidal ideation, it's safe to

---

[5] Bobadilla, Leonardo. "Martyrdom redefined: Self-destructive killers and vulnerable narcissism." *Behavioral and brain sciences* 37, no. 4 (2014): 364.

[6] Weisbrot, Deborah M. "Prelude to a school shooting? Assessing threatening behaviors in childhood and adolescence." *Journal of the American Academy of Child & Adolescent Psychiatry* 47, no. 8 (2008): 847-852.

## Chapter Two: The Usual Suspects

say, the threat of violent assault increases exponentially.

Having said all that, however, on a fundamental level, the mental state and motives of mass shooters must be distinguished from psychiatric diagnoses. Accordingly, severe mental health problems are behind less than 30% of active shooter attacks. In other words, while mental illness is a contributing factor, it is not the cause of mass shootings. We should be careful not to perpetuate the myth that mental illness leads to gun violence.

Motive is also a key distinguishing factor. Meta-analysis suggests two main motives for mass shootings: Desire for fame or revenge. According to scholarly consensus, notoriety, fame and celebrity like attention is a central motive for mass shootings. The prevalence of this may be understood, for example, when children are asked about the most important thing for their future. In a recent survey, the most common answer is "to be famous." Whereas people from previous generations placed a premium on being contributing members of society and gaining success, the 2007 Pew Research survey found that 50% of Americans aged 18–25 say that "to be famous" is one of their most important goals.

Arguably, because notoriety is premium, the distinction between fame and infamy is becoming blurred. For instance, some 20% of millennials say they would forego having a family and children for the possibility of fame.[7] That the media and movies help boost the narrative that notoriety is "it" may be demonstrated by how criminals, serial killers, and bank robbers often achieve celebrity status. In fact, as argued by Adam Lankford and James Silver, "social media has become a competitive battlefield for people who will say or post anything to get noticed. Overall, many people have become so desperate for attention that they would rather get negative attention than feel like they are being ignored. An active shooter with this motive wants to be recognized, not to mention create fear and panic, and inflict as much damage as possible; "burn, kill, and destroy" (Nikolas Cruz).

Many active shooters kill believing that murdering others is the way to resolve their distress in life. In light of the media coverage that is sure to come about, many active shooters, especially those with the motive of fame, tend to kill as a result of their desire to "make the news." For instance, according to Peter Langman, Eric Harris (Columbine shooter) was so desperate for status, he saw murder and suicide as his tickets to everlasting fame, as it said on his website, "I want to leave an impression on the world." Explaining such a mindset, Langman observes, "by dying in the attack, he (Harris) found a way out of a meaningless existence at the same time he achieved world fame."[8]

---

[7] Lankford, Adam. "Public mass shooters and firearms: A cross-national study of 171 countries." *Violence and victims* 31, no. 2 (2016): 187-199.
[8] Peter Langman, *Why Kids Kill: Inside the Minds of School Shooters* (New York: Macmillan, 2009), 132.

## Chapter Two: The Usual Suspects

Regarding revenge as a motive, as previously said, mass shooters often see themselves as victims of injustice, and are thus motivated by revenge or power. Citing a now famous example, it is clear that Eric Harris and Darren Klebold were primarily motivated by vengeance against their real or supposed oppressors. It may be argued, an active shooter with the desire for revenge views the media limelight as fulfilling their subconscious need for validation. These disturbed children felt inadequate. Particularly, as observed by Peter Langman, to overcome this obstacle, they wrongly believed that "violence enhances the social standing of males." As Langman has argued, mass shooters believed they could use violence to enhance their status and achieve lasting fame. Accordingly, common factors include: "Homicidal rage, suicidal anguish, inadequate identities seeking to establish an image of manliness through violence, envy toward those of higher status, a desire for fame, fragile personalities that are highly reactive to commonplace slights and frustrations, and a masochistic tendency to hold grudges and magnify wrongs suffered."[9]

### Societal Variables

Adding to these factors, there are likewise various societal variables to the phenomenon of mass

---

[9] Ibid., 209.

shootings. These may be defined as media/movie violence, media coverage, and the Copy Cat Effect.

Generally speaking, it may be said there is an American fascination with, and tendency toward violence in entertainment. In his book *On Killing*, Dave Grossman argues that violent content in video games, movies and media teach children to kill. In the past few decades there has been a proliferation of violence in movies. Likewise, video games have become increasingly realistic and violent.

For instance, the game *Grand Theft Auto IV* allows you to murder anything that walks as well as have sex with prostitutes. This issue takes center stage as we consider that violent video games were contributing element in the Columbine and Virginia Tech mass shootings. Eric Harris wrote, "I have been playing Doom since November 1994. It is basically my life. I live in this place." He went so far as to say, "I wish I lived in Doom. I have a goal to destroy as much as possible." From this statement what may be understood is, violence in a virtual world may surface in the real world. It stands to reason that Grossman's argument is valid. The burden of proof lies with the one who would argue otherwise. Unfortunely, Grossman's concern has largely gone unaddressed.

Perhaps the most virulent societal variable in this discussion is the coalescence of media coverage and what is called The Copy Cat Effect. In her book *The Copycat Effect*, Loren Coleman convincingly argues

## Chapter Two: The Usual Suspects

that media coverage triggers more mass shootings. For example, she sites how mass shootings steadily increased in 1990s and then proliferated in the limelight of non-stop media coverage of the 1999 Columbine High School shooting. There were three more school shootings in 1999, six in 2000, and five in 2001. Then came the 911 attacks. Tellingly, observes Coleman, "Before September 11, 2001, media attention seemed focused on what school shooting might be next. When the terrorist attack occurred, a virtual media blackout kept other violence out of the news. But, in fact there were no shooting rampages in American schools during the entire scholastic year of 2001-2002. Little did the media notice or comment on the fact that school shootings had decreased so precipitously when they weren't reporting on them."[10]

The point is, mass shootings lead to other mass shootings. The sensationalized news reporting creates "anti-hero" figures out of mass shooters. This in turn appeals to others who have considered undertaking mass shootings themselves. When it comes to school shootings, there are essentially three fatal ingredients: There's a disturbed child, the "promise" of media coverage, and an American fascination with violence. Then, in the majority of mass shootings, there were clearly identified

---

[10] Loren Coleman, *The Copycat Effect: How the Media and Popular Culture Trigger the Mayhem in Tomorrow's Headlines* (New York: Simon and Schuster, 2004), 179.

triggering events which caused intolerable distress that pushed individuals into action – making their fantasies become a reality.

Studies show that active shooters aren't concerned with dying and so have nothing to lose. They expect to die. Statistically, they are apprehended or eliminated within the first five minutes of the incident. They will move through a building or area until they're either stopped by others, stopped by police or commit suicide, or assisted suicide by law enforcement.

According to the FBI, about 70% of active shooter incidents end with the shooter or shooters' deaths. However, unlike a homicide or mass killing, the "active" aspect implies that both law enforcement and citizens have the potential to affect the outcome of the event. We now move to discuss the type of decision-making required in an active shooter situation.

The main findings of the FBI study included the following: The vast majority of shootings (70%) occurred in either a place of business or an educational environment (these figures exclude shootings related to gang or drug violence). Most shootings were carried out by a single individual. The shooter committed suicide 40% of the time. Moreover, most incidents (67%) ended before police even arrived and could engage the perpetrator.

## Chapter Two: The Usual Suspects

### Common Threat Characteristics

Tellingly, some 75% of those who participated in mass violence exhibited signs beforehand. While the following factors alone do not indicate that an individual will commit a violent act, these characteristics have been commonly associated with past perpetrators of active shooter incidents:

1. *Disgruntled employee* – The disgruntled employee is most likely a white male in his 30s or 40s, may have prior military service, lives alone, and may possess an antisocial or asocial personality. Contrary to general impressions, lethal employees rarely have a violent criminal record and are unlikely to have undergone psychiatric treatment. A textbook example was DeWayne Craddock. On May 31, 2019, this disgruntled city employee fatally shot 12 people and wounded 4 others. Before this Virginia Beach shooter was shot dead by responding police officers, he had no criminal record. Further, they are not likely to be drug users. In many instances, shooters are often motivated by revenge and anger over job termination, disagreement with job performance evaluation, or long-term arguments with coworkers.

2. *Paranoid and delusional students* – As argued, school shooters often harbor anger and paranoid delusions, have low self-esteem and hang out with an outcast group. Independent studies by the FBI, Secret Service, and Department of Education offer several insights on shootings committed by students. Like

their adult counterparts, these students are often male, may be struggling with academic performance, have had conflicts with teachers or peers, and are described as loners.

There is usually a triggering event, either a lost job or a falling out with a girlfriend that finally makes them snap. They also tend to be obsessed with guns, violent video games or movies. In retrospect, investigators uncover warning signs, such as trying to recruit a peer or writing hateful stories. In many cases, students actually come out and say exactly what they're going to do.

*3. Intended victims* – While victims can be chosen indiscriminately, management personnel are frequently targeted. Studies have shown that over 65% of workplace homicides involve the death of a supervisor, manager, or employer. Active shooters view the attack as an attempt to correct a perceived wrong. They usually have a "hit list" and will search these victims out and often take-out targets of opportunity on the way.

*4. Weapons used* – Regarding weapons, 59% of active shooters have perpetrated their crimes with a pistol and 26% with a rifle (AR-15 type). The remainder is with a shotgun or knife. Moreover, analysis demonstrates that 36% of attacks involved more than one weapon. And in many cases, the attackers used firearms that they had stolen from relatives or friends.

## Chapter Two: The Usual Suspects

Pre-attack signs include what is referred to as "leakage." This is warning behavior or any communication to a third party of the intent to do harm.[11] In roughly 80% of all school attacks, someone had prior knowledge of the attacker's plan.

Beyond these characteristics, however, there are few commonalities among mass shooters. This can make it difficult to weed out an employee or student who's just having a bad day and one who might act on their grievances.

### *Summary*

In light of this, there are several implications. First, there is no single "profile" of an active shooter. They are not always readily identifiable prior to the attack. Second, many have pointed to gun laws as the perpetrator, arguing that stricter laws on guns would lead to less violent crimes. However, gun laws alone cannot be argued as a factor in this sense. Besides, firearm deaths by suicide account for the majority of yearly gun-related deaths. Third, mass shootings by people with serious mental illness remain exceedingly rare events and represent a fraction of a percent of all yearly gun-related homicides. Fourth, as the media hype surrounding mass shootings continue, we can only expect many more. It is not too tinfoil-hatted to

---

[11] Meloy, J. R., & O'Toole, M. E. (2011). The concept of leakage in threat assessment. Behavioral Sciences & the Law, 29, 513–527. http://dx.doi.org/10.1002/bsl.986

say this trend is indicative of a larger moral implosion on a national level. Though a look into this is out of the present scope of this book, it's safe to say that what we're experiencing in America, as well as western civilization as a whole, is a disintegration of society's foundation. We need a moral compass correction. Only a fool thinks these events will stop without one.

In the last analysis, the phenomenon of mass shootings in the United States is likely a result of a combination of the previously mentioned factors, including various sociocultural ones that must be better understood if these tragedies are to be prevented.

# 3

## Decisive Action: Detect, Deny, Defend

*"The only thing necessary for the triumph of evil is for good men to do nothing."* — Edmund Burke

So far, we have surveyed various aspects of situational awareness (SA), how it enables us to better detect a threat. We have discussed various contributing factors as to why mass shootings occur. Our goal in this chapter is to lay out the framework of decisive action, the paradigm of detect, deny, and defend. Before we do, it's important to understand the way our brain works when encountering a threat.

When we encounter a threat, our brain commands a response from the body that is instantly executed. Our sympathetic nervous system (SNS) reacts by releasing hormones into our body and extra blood to our muscles that we will need to survive. First, our brain processes the information through sensory organs in the amygdala and hippocampus. The amygdala sees the significance of what's going on and alerts the brain (observe). The hippocampus, which stores emotional memory, then categorizes and filters the threat through an emotional lens to evaluate it (orient).

Receiving input from the hippocampus, the cingulate cortex makes a decision, activating the hypothalamus-pituitary-adrenal (HPA) - axis. This results in the release of "powerful stress hormones, including cortisol and adrenaline, which increase heart rate, blood pressure, and rate of breathing, preparing us to fight back or run away."[1] Adrenaline payout gives us a huge surge in energy. Our body follows up with cortisol for continued alertness.

This whole process takes a matter of seconds. Ultimately, we'll react to a threat in either one of three ways: Halting in place, moving away from the threat, or preparing to physically engage the threat. These three responses are often referred to as the "freeze, flight, or fight" responses. As Paul Howe observes:

> When the sound of shots ring out, the average person will stop and cringe physically and mentally. As soon as they register what the shots actually are – i.e., gunfire – their fight-or-flight response will kick in. For the average human, the urge is to flee.[2]

What causes a person to respond in either of these ways? It stands to reason, if you believe you can eliminate the attacker, you will move to meet the threat. But if you believe there's no hope of defeating the attacker, your inclination will be to run. If you respond by freezing, it means you are overwhelmed by events and cannot make a decision. The worst thing to do is freeze.

---

[1] Bessel A. Van der Kolk, *The Body Keeps the Score: Brain, Mind, And Body in The Healing of Trauma* (New York: Penguin Books, 2015), 61.
[2] Paul Howe, *Leadership and Training for the Fight* (New York: Skyhorse, 2011), 11.

# Chapter Three: Decisive Action: Detect, Deny, Defend

## The OODA Loop

As has been said, we have to know what we're looking for, then put that information into context, making it actionable. Perhaps the best cognitive system for doing just that is John Boyd's OODA Loop. The OODA Loop is a learning system and decision-making process that was first laid out by US Air Force fighter pilot and military strategist Colonel John Boyd. The four steps are Observe, Orient, Decide, Act. John Boyd studied a wide range of historic battles. From his research, he concluded that where numerically inferior forces had defeated their opponents, they often did so by presenting the other side with a sudden, unexpected change or a series of changes.

According to Boyd, these superior forces fell victim because they could not adjust to the changes in a timely manner. Generally, defeat came at relatively small cost to the victor. This research led to Boyd's decision cycle theory, which states that conflict may be viewed as time-competitive cycles of observation, orientating, deciding, and acting (OODA).

Situational awareness is a mental process, and the goal is to determine and implement the first solution that could result in success. In context, in a violent confrontation, the one who can cycle through the OODA Loop the fastest wins (See figure 3-1).

As Boyd explained, as we move through our decision or time-competitive cycle, the goal is to travel through the Loop faster than our opponent so that they fall behind, paralyzed by their inability to analyze the situation. As is apparent, time is the key factor in the decision cycle.

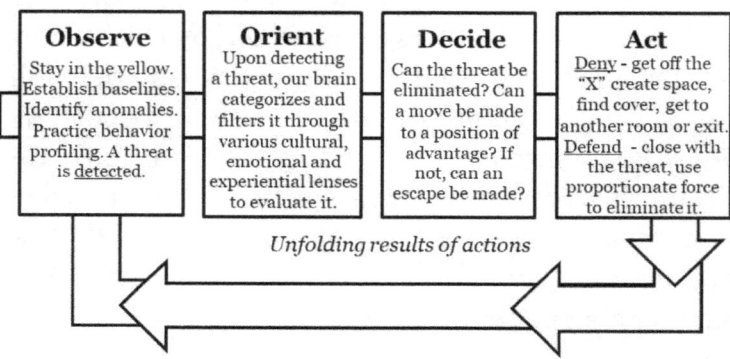

Figure 3-1. Decision Cycle.

An example of the time-competitive cycle comes to us from aerial combat during the Korean War: Aviators achieved a high kill ratio of about 10:1 over their North Korean and Chinese opponents. At first glance, this is somewhat surprising. The main enemy fighter, the MiG-15, was superior to the American F-86 in a number of key respects. It could climb and accelerate faster, and it had a better sustained turn rate. The F-86, however, was superior to the MiG in two critical, though less obvious, respects. First, because it had high-powered hydraulic controls, the F-86 could shift from one maneuver to another faster

# Chapter Three: Decisive Action: Detect, Deny, Defend

than the MiG. Second, because of its bubble canopy, the F-86 pilot had better visibility. The F-86's better field of view provided better situational awareness and also contributed to fast transitions because it allowed its pilot to understand changing situations more quickly.

American pilots developed new tactics based on these two advantages. When they engaged the MiGs, they sought to put them through a series of maneuvers. The F-86's faster transitions between maneuvers gave it a time advantage that the pilot transformed into a position advantage. Often, when the MiG pilots realized what was happening, they panicked—and thereby made the American pilot's job all the easier.[3]

Crucial to the time-competitive cycle is that once the process begins, it mustn't slow down. It must continue and must accelerate. As Robert Coram observes, "Success is the greatest trap for the novice who properly implements the OODA Loop. He is so amazed at what he has done that he pauses and looks around and waits for reinforcements. But this is the time to exploit the confusion and to press on."[4] Thus, as we've seen, the art of making decisions rapidly, depends upon our ability to recognize patterns and then intuitively and aggressively act.

---

[3] MCDP 1-3 Tactics, 68.
[4] Coram, *Boyd: The Fighter Pilot Who Changed the Art of War*, 338.

## Active Shooter Awareness and Response

As Boyd would tell us, it's often the ability to make good decisions quickly and execute them within our opponent's decision cycle that determines who wins. Making decisions rapidly, enables one to enter an opponent's decision cycle as he is merely reacting to conditions as they occur. Then, recognizing fleeting opportunities, and preventing the opponent from reorganizing, and pushing him to make mistakes, decisive results can be achieved.

Physiologically, an essential aspect to our survival that is often overlooked involves controlling our emotions, namely fear. Fear can overwhelm a person. If left unchecked, fear can control you. To survive a deadly encounter, you need to be confident in your own abilities and control fear. Physiology also plays an important role as in a deadly encounter. A person's heart rate rises and they begin to lose fine and gross motor skills. With this mind, a key factor is knowing your strengths and weaknesses so that over time, your body will be trained to react subconsciously.

The type of decision-making required in an active shooter situation is rapid. Our goal is to make a rapid decision and then execute it quickly and aggressively. Arguably, there are essentially two types of decision-making: analytical and intuitive. Analytical decision-making works in situations in which we have sufficient time to problem solve, plan, and deliberate options. The reality is that we don't use this approach for the majority of decisions we make on a daily basis.

## Chapter Three: Decisive Action: Detect, Deny, Defend

If we did, we would never get through the day. As has been said, most active shooter situations are over in less than five minutes; the first few seconds is crucial. Analytical decision-making is therefore neither practical nor useful in high-stress situations.

When we don't have the luxury of time, intuitive decision-making, which is based on intuition, involves critically assessing information. This type of decision making involves collecting and weeding out the unimportant information and focus on the important. Intuition is your brain's way of processing information and nudging you in a way that bypasses your conscious brain.

Intuition is nothing more than a person's sense about a situation influenced by experience and knowledge. It's the way the mind picks up on patterns and uses experience and knowledge, guiding us to make a decision. It's rightly called a "gut feeling," since people can literally have a physical response when their intuition tries to make them aware of something they do not consciously know. The point is, perfect decisions aren't possible.

Recalling the imperative of staying "left of bang," the key is to recognize anomalies. Spot things that are out of place. Determine a person's intentions based on human behavior, and filter out irrelevant information. We should also know the layout of the room we're in, the exits, and where we could go in trouble (mental map). Our brain must register what is happening before a response kicks in. If we are "in the white," and an active shooter interrupts our family's outing, we run a great risk of sacrificing our loved ones on the altar of our unpreparedness.

The type of decision-making required in an active shooter situation is rapid. Our goal is to make a rapid decision and then execute it quickly and aggressively. Our goal is to devise a 70% solution and act violently and quickly to carry it out.

With these three responses of freeze, flight or fight in mind, there have been several methodologies developed to help people deal with such violent confrontations, two are especially prevalent: "Run, Hide, Fight," and "Avoid, Deny, Defend." This book adopts the second paradigm and incorporates it into a broader decisive action methodology to facing active shooter situations.

### *Detect – Deny – Defend*

In the military, when soldiers are suddenly attacked, for example in an ambush, they are taught to "get off the X." Most importantly, getting off the "X" gets you out of the area where most of the firepower will be directed. Secondly, getting off the "X" creates space and optimally gives you room to maneuver and engage the threat. While not denigrating the "run, hide, fight" paradigm, "detect, deny, defend" emphasizes a proactive mindset which puts us on better footing. Ultimately, your best

## Chapter Three: Decisive Action: Detect, Deny, Defend

defense is a good offensive mindset. There are three aspects of the paradigm: Detect – Deny – Defend (See figure 3-2).

**Detect** – As a hunter, we look for wolves, and remain at a heightened sense of awareness (yellow). Detect starts with your state of mind; maintaining SA and knowing your surroundings. When we enter any building, we should quickly familiarize our self with the layout. We should note at least two exits out of the room/building we are in. We should note areas of the building we could potentially run to for either cover or shelter. We should consider the construction type of the walls. Could they stop a bullet? We should note potential weapons, i.e., fire extinguishers, kitchen knives, chairs, etc. (even if we are armed).

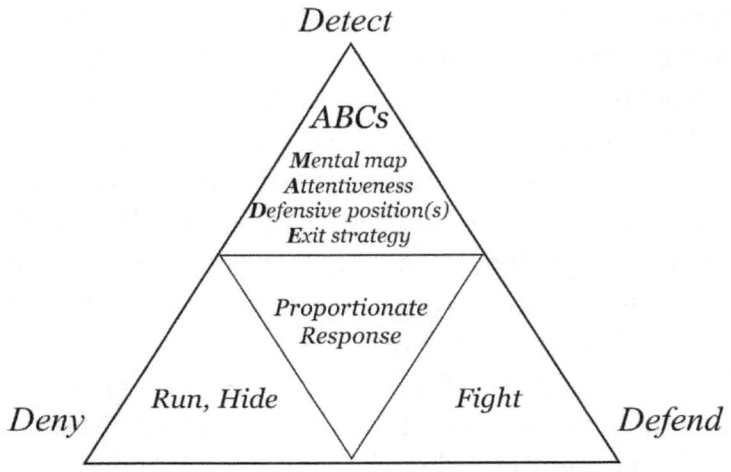

Figure 3-2. Decisive Action: Avoid, Deny, Defend

We need an exit strategy, a way to move away from the threat and off the "X" as quickly as possible. We need to have an escape route in mind. We should evacuate regardless of whether others agree to follow. If possible, alert others onsite with an intercom, phone, page, or the "code." Leave your belongings behind. Help others escape, and if possible, prevent others from entering an area where the active shooter may be. The more distance and barriers between you and the threat, the better.

Many advocate compliance. In other words, do what the shooter says. However, an active shooter doesn't want to talk, they want to kill. Compliance is therefore not an option.

**Deny** – They say prevention is the best cure. However proactive we may be, there's no demographic profile for active shooters, and there's no pattern or method to the selection of their victims. Moreover, we can't always have the best seat in a restaurant, building, office, etc. And so, getting away may prove to be difficult or might be even impossible. If that's the case, the goal is still to create space – get off the "X," as much as possible. Is escape the best option? Where is the shooter? Multiple shooters? Can you get out immediately undetected? Can the threat be eliminated? If not, the goal is to maximize the distance between you and the threat.

The first option to deny is run. You don't need doors and traditional entrances and exits to a building to

## Chapter Three: Decisive Action: Detect, Deny, Defend

make your escape. If you are on the first floor and the windows can open to an escape, take it. Leave your belongings behind; these will only slow you down. The active shooter is not interested in taking your items. He wants to take your life. These items can be replaced. Run as far away from the building and/or area as possible. Stay away from windows. When it is safe to do so call 911. Try to get the attention of others who appear to be entering the building but are unaware of the crisis.

If you cannot exit the building, attempt to create barriers to prevent or slow down a threat from getting to you and others. This is the hide option. You should have already familiarized yourself with options – places within the building/room to run to for cover or shelter.

Run to a part of the building you can barricade yourself and others in. If the door has a lock, lock it. If the door is equipped with a "self-closing" arm that is at the top of the door, secure the two arms together by using a belt, cord, long purse strap, or any binding material to make the door difficult to open. Work with others to make this happen. Seconds become minutes.

Add to the barricade. Use desks, cabinets and other furniture to place against the door to make entry more difficult. If you have multiple desks or tables in a room, line them up from the door to the wall opposite the door to make a "brace" that prevents entry. If it's possible to safely exit through a window, do it. Don't block this exit point. Turn off the lights. If the door has a window blind, lower it. If possible lower or close window blinds to allow as little of outdoor light to come in the room. Make the room as dark as possible.

Any little noise can tip off an active shooter. Silence your cell phone. Don't huddle in one part of the room. You will only be making everyone a bigger target. Spread out throughout the room and remain outside the line of sight. Try to find cover behind large objects in the room.

Remain quiet. You may be in a room with a person who is overcome with fear. Console this person and dial 911. Provide as much information as possible, giving such things as location of the shooter, physical description of the shooter, and number of people injured. Chapter ten discusses this more in depth.

**Defend** – As Americans, we have a constitutional right to defend ourselves. We have the right to use reasonable or defensive force, for the purpose of defending our own life and the lives of others, including, if the situation warrants, the use of deadly force. In chapter seven, we will take a more in-depth look at self-defense. At this stage of the situation, we'll be either proactive or reactive. If a threat has warranted the focus of our attention from a potential threat to a potential target, we may draw our weapon if the potential target's actions dictate such a response.

## Chapter Three: Decisive Action: Detect, Deny, Defend

Take for example, the actions of an off-duty police officer who blunted a killing spree. On May 27, 2010, seventy-nine-year-old Abraham Dickan, walked into an AT&T store with the intent to murder six of the company's employees. He began his attack by firing his .357 Magnum at the store employee who was working the front counter. Before he could complete his assault, he was shot dead by an off-duty Rome police officer who happened to be in the store shopping. Before the police officer placed killing shots on this active shooter, he considered the fourth cardinal rule of weapon's safety: Know your target, what's around it and behind it. In other words, he checked the background (behind the active shooter) for innocent bystanders before he fired. In this situation, the policer officer's aggressive and decisive action prevented a greater loss of life to senseless slaughter.

Another clear example of defend was the thwarted active shooter attack by Floyd Corkins on August 15, 2012 at the Family Research Council in Washington, DC. Corkins, wielding a 9mm pistol along with two magazines and 50 rounds of ammunition, entered the lobby of Family Research Council's Washington, D.C. headquarters. He shot an employee, 46-year-old Leonardo Johnson, in the left arm. While injured, Johnson assisted others who wrestled the gunman to the ground until police arrived and placed the gunman under arrest. Johnson's aggressive and decisive action prevented a greater loss of life.

If we have run away from the active shooter and barricaded ourselves, we need to be prepared for a possible entry of the shooter. If unarmed, look for things in the room that could be used as weapons such as scissors, a letter knife, chairs, a printer, books, or fire extinguisher, etc. Remember, there is safety in numbers. Upon entry of the shooter, commit 100% to the fight. Attack the shooter by throwing heavy objects. Do whatever it takes to disarm the shooter and incapacitate him to neutralize the situation.

### *Summary*

If you can't run or hide, you must be prepared to defend yourself and others. In active shooter situations, actions determine survivability. Actions have to be decisive, rapid, and violent. Its best to be proactive and aggressive rather than passive. You have to commit 100%. In the next three chapters we'll discuss how this all plays out when life is on the line.

# 4

## Active Shooter Awareness and Response in Businesses

*"Our world is no longer a safe and predictable place. We cannot allow ourselves to be pulled into a false sense of security. Today's tragedy is a stark reminder that we are not immune from these types of domestic terror attacks nor the hateful motives which drive these assailants."* – Sheriff Sadie Darnell

Since Columbine, four out of ten mass shootings occur in businesses. One of the worst mass killings in history occurred in a place where people were celebrating life. In the early morning hours of June 12, 2016, Pulse, a prominent gay nightclub located in Orlando, Florida was holding a "Latin" night. At about 2:01 a.m., Omar Seddique Mateen (from here on out to be known as the shooter) entered the club armed with a pistol and an assault rifle (Sig Sauer MCX) and began systematically murdering those inside. Starting at the dance floor, the shooter fired round after round into the bodies of those scrambling for their lives.

As the music was pounding, some mistook the gunshots for firecrackers or just part of the music. One clubgoer describing the scene said, "All hell broke loose." Running for the doors, some made it while others were gunned down. Some were wounded and played dead on the dance floor, still others barricaded themselves inside bathroom stalls. Alerted to the sounds of gunfire, the security guard, off-duty cop Adam Gruler, engaged the shooter and called for backup. Unscathed, the shooter made another deadly sweep through the club, stopping only when his assault rifle jammed. With pistol in hand, the shooter went after those in the bathrooms, killing more there. After firing hundreds of rounds, the shooter paused to search for news coverage of his attack on his phone. He also googled the spelling of "allegiance" and checked for ways to clear his jammed rifle. Then, calling 911, he professed his allegiance to Abu Bakr al-Baghdadi of the Islamic State (ISIS). Calling 911 a total of five times, the shooter falsely claimed that he had placed a bomb in one of the cars parked outside, and said that he was wearing an explosive vest, the kind he said that "was used in France." During his 911 conversations he also said that the Tsarnaev brothers, who attacked the Boston Marathon in 2012, were his "homeboys."

Two hours into the attack, at 4:21 a.m., police were able to assist some of the survivors in escaping through a hole in the outer wall of the club's dressing rooms. As 5 a.m. approached, those inside lying wounded and bleeding called police from their cellphones. Then, at around 5:02 am, the police crashed through the outer wall of the building with an armored car, allowing the rest of the hostages to escape. The shooter then engaged police through the

## Chapter Five: Awareness and Response in Businesses

hole in the outer wall and was met by a hail of fire from law enforcement and was brought down. When the smoked cleared, this senseless hate crime claimed the lives of 49 innocent people, injured more than 50 others, and left a scar on a community.

In light of the shooter's professing allegiance to ISIS, one of the curious things about this senseless attack was that it was perpetrated by a first-generation American, born to Afghan Muslim parents. As touching motive, what may be known from the shooter's father is that he was enraged having seen two gay men kiss. Curiously, however, multiple media outlets reported that some Pulse regular clubgoers recognized Mateen and said he had frequented the nightclub as a patron. Allegedly, Mateen had been known to interact with at least two men from the club on gay dating apps.

There are many other details as well as much speculation. For example, there is speculation regarding whether police fired indiscriminately into the club. However, a formal investigation into the attack officially cleared the officers involved from any wrong doing. When this attack is analyzed with other senseless massacres, a common denominator is a predictable sequence referred to as an "attack cycle." One of the goals of this chapter is to outline this cycle so as to gain an awareness of preattack signals given off by mass shooters.

*Active Shooter Awareness and Response*

## *Attack Cycle*

It is said that criminal activity normally follows a predictable pattern. This is underscored by the fact that as high as 90% of victim's recall noticing suspicious activity prior to the crime. In 2018, the FBI released an analysis entitled "A Study of the Pre-Attack Behaviors of Active Shooters in the United States Between 2000 and 2013." This comprehensive study examines motives and observable pre-attack behaviors. Three key behaviors are as follows:

*1. Threats made.* Over 40% of active shooters had previously made verbal or written threats. Yet these exchanges were either ignored or undocumented. Before shooters actually kill, they usually assault, abuse or threaten people close to them, such as spouses or co-workers. They are often profoundly alienated from society. Omar Mateen, who committed the Orlando shooting, routinely beat his first wife, threatened co-workers and could barely hold down a job. Likewise, prior to the attack on First Baptist Church of Sutherland Springs, the shooter sent threatening texts.

Even those shooters without violent histories, such as Dylann Roof (Emmanuel AME Church shooting) or Seung-Hui Cho (Virginia Tech shooting), were known by friends, family or teachers to make disturbing threats and had withdrawn from normal social life. Tellingly, according to the FBI study, when

## Chapter Five: Awareness and Response in Businesses

others observed concerning behavior in these active shooters, more than half took no action at all. The implication here is attack cycle indicators could include noticing a person making threats towards specific people or places in general conversation. Such threats should be taken seriously.

*2. Became obsessed and idolized previous shooters.* As we discovered in chapter 2, many mass shooters want to be "famous." It was apparent that the Pulse night club shooter idolized the recent Boston Marathon (2012) and Paris attacks (2015). He seemed to have attempted to emulate at least the explosive vest and bomb littered aspects of both attacks. Likewise, Seung-Hui Cho, the perpetrator of the Virginia Tech massacre, idolized the Columbine shooters and appears to have gone to school on them. It is therefore not too tinfoil-hatted to say that media coverage plays a prominent role.

*3. Planning was involved.* According to the FBI study, 77% of active shooters spent a week or longer planning their attack. Regarding attack planning, it may be safely argued there are three such groups. These consist of a "focused shooter," a "spree-type shooter," and an "incoherently-focused shooter." Focused shooters, like those who perpetrated the Columbine, Virginia Tech, and the Sutherland Springs shootings undertook extensive planning, including pre-operational surveillance. Preparations may even be virtual. For example, the video games Doom and Duke Nukem provided extensive dress rehearsals for the Columbine shooters by allowing them to mentally rehearse the rampage.[1]

Additionally, a few active shooters even set up pre-planned defenses intended to trap victims and prolong their attacks, such as chaining doors and blocking entrances as in Virginia Tech. Accordingly, metrics show that in 7 out of 10 incidents, the shooter planned the attack and was therefore focused.

However, some shooters do little to no planning and attack impulsively. On July 18, 1984, James Oliver Huberty opened fire in a crowded McDonald's restaurant in San Ysidro, California, killing 21 people and wounding 19 others. Armed with several semi-automatic weapons, Huberty had left home, telling his wife, "I'm going hunting...hunting for humans." Huberty, who had a history of mental problems, lost his job a month before the shootings. His wife claimed that he called a mental health clinic to make an appointment for counseling. Reprehensibly, he was never called back. An hour after the shooting began, a member of San Diego SWAT brought the incident to an end by shooting Huberty in the chest, killing him.

In a similar fashion, those enjoying their lunches were terrorized as George Hennard drove his truck

---

[1] Peter Langman, *Why Kids Kill: Inside the Minds of School Shooters* (New York: MacMillan, 2009), 5.

## Chapter Five: Awareness and Response in Businesses

through the front window of the Luby's Cafeteria in Killen, Texas. The shooter stepped out of the truck, pulled out a pistol and began firing into the restaurant's patrons. As recounted in an interview, Suzanna Gratia Hupp always prided herself on being a law-abiding citizen, but she regrets that she obeyed what was then Texas law on Oct. 16, 1991. While she and her parents Al and Ursula were there with her that day, Hupp, reached for her purse where she kept a handgun for self-defense.

The shooter was about 15 feet away but she then realized she left her gun in her car. As she recounts, "A few months earlier, I had chosen to obey the law and leave my gun in the car. When the realization sunk in, I thought, Great. What do I do now?" Hupp's father was shot as he attempted to charge the gunman. Then someone smashed a window, creating an escape route. Hupp went through the window and called back to her mother to follow, not realizing that her mother was already mortally wounded. Before the shooter was brought down by law enforcement, he had killed 23 people and wounded 27 others. This event prompted then Texas Governor George W. Bush to make it legal for Texans to carry a concealed gun.

In passing, a few observations may be made regarding this attack. First, there were three basic responses to the active shooter – run, hide, or fight. Due to the close proximity of the shooter, having driven into the restaurant, surprise was complete. In this incident, it seems the best chances of survival followed those who escaped through windows and doors. Second, it goes without saying that an armed citizen could have blunted this attack. Third, this incident underscores the fact that such senseless attacks can happen any place where there are concentrations of people.

On February 2007, Kenneth Hammond, an off-duty police officer, was out on an early Valentine's Day dinner with his wife when he encountered a gunman in a mall. Eighteen-year-old Sulejman Talovic had entered Trolley Square Mall in Salt Lake City armed with a shotgun and a backpack full of ammunition. With the help of another officer, Hammond drew his weapon and confronted a shooter who had opened fire in a shopping mall, killing five before being fatally shot. Talovic wanted "to kill a large number of people" and probably would have had it not been for these police officers.

However, there are anomalies. The deadliest mass shooting in US history occurred on October 1, 2017 when Sixty-four-year-old Stephen Paddock fired into a crowd of 20,000 people attending the Route 91 musical festival in Las Vegas. This senseless attack killed 60 people and wounding 867. As law enforcement made entry into his hotel suite, Paddock committed suicide.

## Chapter Five: Awareness and Response in Businesses

In a similar manner, James Holmes killed 12 people and wounded 58 when he opened fire during a midnight showing of "The Dark Knight Rises." Along with other patrons, Holmes waited in line and entered the Century 16 movie theater in Aurora, Colorado on July 20, 2012. About thirty minutes into the film, he exited the theater through the exit door that went immediately outside, propping it open, then returned armed with four weapons, body armor and a gas mask. Holmes threw smoke canisters and opened fire into the unsuspecting audience. Twelve additional people were injured in the scramble to escape. When Holmes was later arrested in his car, he told police he was "The Joker." Holmes also booby-trapped his apartment which police were able to safely dismantle. He is currently serving a life sentence.

While extensive planning was evident in both of these heinous attacks, motives remain unknown. Mass shootings of this nature would seem to fall into the category of incoherently-focused. Both Holmes and Paddock purchased their firearms legally. Moreover, that both murders had a certain focus is demonstrated by the fact in the firearms that had on hand to do the evil deed; Paddock had an arsenal of some 23 weapons. In terms of survivor actions, the best option in both of these attacks was to get off the "X."

This demonstrates a shooter's decision to act isn't a knee-jerk reaction. There is often a trigger event –

such as a heated argument, poor review, or termination – that motivates the shooter. However, the length of time between the final straw and the mass shooting could be days or months. Tellingly, in about half the instances, the shooter had been fired from work and returned months later to settle a score.

A textbook case that demonstrates this was the Atlanta Day Trade massacre. In July 1999, Mark Barton killed his wife and children before going on a shooting spree at two different office complexes where he worked, killing 12 people and wounding 13. While firing his .45 and 9mm pistols, the shooter said, "I hope this doesn't ruin your trading day." In the previous two months, Barton had suffered some $105,000 in losses day trading and was fired in April. After fleeing the scene, Barton killed himself before he could be apprehended by police.

Another key finding of the FBI study is the fact that active shooters often attack people and places with which they were already familiar. Understandably then, only some 14% approached or conducted surveillance prior to their attack.

### *Could Be A Case of Mistaken Identity*

Active shooter incidents can be as confusing as they are dangerous. On January 8, 2011, Representative Gabrielle Giffords and 18 others were shot when Jared Lee Loughner opened fire outside a supermarket in Casas Adobes, Arizona. Ms. Giffords

## Chapter Five: Awareness and Response in Businesses

was holding a meeting with constituents. Loughner had exhibited increasingly strange behavior in recent months. On the morning of the shooting, he posted the following on MySpace page, "Goodbye. Dear friends. Please don't be mad at me." Giffords was believed to be the target of assassination. Walking up behind her, the gunman shot her in the head, and then continued shooting.

After his initial salvo, the shooter began to reload and two bystanders wrestled him to the ground. As the shooting began, Joe Zamudio was in a nearby drugstore. Armed, he ran to the scene. As Zamudio accounts, "I came out of that store, I clicked the safety off, and I was ready." Upon seeing the man with the gun, who was not Loughner, Zamudio grabbed his arm and shoved him into a wall. Realizing he wasn't the shooter, Zamudio didn't engage. That's how close he came to killing an innocent man. Among the 18 people shot, six were killed. Incredibly, Giffords survived. The two men who wrestled Loughner to the ground prevented him from taking more lives.

### *Summary*

In light of the afore mentioned preattack indicators, a few implications may be made. First, its everyone's responsibility to take such threats seriously. In light of preattack signs and behavior, if you recognize it but take no action, the opportunity for intervention is lost. Second, co-workers and students who make threats against others should be regarded as risks, even months or years after their departure. Third, there is no single warning sign, or checklist for identifying "preattack behaviors." However, it is possible to prevent some attacks through effective threat assessment and management strategies. This aspect will be covered in chapter 11.

# 5

## Active Shooter Awareness and Response in Schools

*"Together Americans have overcome many evils and found strength through many storms."* – President George W. Bush

Perhaps more so than other mass shooting events, those perpetrated at schools seem to be more emotionally charged, and in the aftermath, the school and its victims are often leveraged by politicians, activists, and the media to further a particular agenda.

On August 1, 1966, Charles Whitman, a former Marine, carried rifles and other weapons to the tower deck of the University of Texas at Austin. He then opened fire, shooting people indiscriminately on the campus. Over a period of 96 minutes Whitman shot and killed 16 people, including an unborn child, and injured 31 others. The attack ended when police officers Ramiro Martinez and Houston McCoy shot him dead. At the time, the attack was the deadliest mass shooting in US History. Sadly, this was surpassed on April 16, 2007.

### Virginia Tech

It was an average Monday morning at Virginia Tech but before lunch, 32 people would be killed and 17 injured in yet another senseless taking of life by a coward with a gun. At 7:15 am, 23-year-old Seung-Hui Cho entered Virginia Tech, the college he was currently attending as a student armed with 9-mm and 22-caliber handguns. The first attack began in the dorms as students were getting ready for classes. Cho shot a female freshman, a woman he may have had a romantic interest in, and a male resident assistant before fleeing the building. Police soon arrived but being unaware of the shooter's identity, they initially pursued the female victim's boyfriend.

Between 9:15 and 9:30 a.m., Cho entered Norris Hall and chained and locked several main doors.[1] Then, armed with two pistols and hundreds of rounds of ammunition, he went from room to room shooting people. Witnesses described scenes of mass chaos and unimaginable horror as some students were lined up against a wall and shot point blank. Responding to 911 calls, police arrived but due to the obstructed entrances, they had to spend five crucial minutes before they could break through.

Amidst the bloodshed, one man laid down his life to save others. In room 204, 76-year-old Liviu Librescu held the door to his classroom shut as he heard shots approaching. Librescu, a holocaust survivor, kept his body pressed against the door as he called for his students to escape through a window.

---

[1] Lucinda Roy, *No Right to Remain Silent: The Tragedy of Virginia Tech* (New York: Harmony Books, 2009), 109.

## Chapter 5: Awareness and Response in Schools

One of his student's recounts, "one moment we were reviewing homework, the next moment we heard the unmistakable pop of gunshots." Jumping free to safety through the window, an eyewitness recounts, "I just remember looking back and seeing him at the door. I don't think I would be here if it wasn't for him." Librescu died a hero as a bullet from Cho's weapon penetrated the door.

About nine minutes into the second attack, police broke through the chain locked door and ran to the sound of the guns. As they approached, Cho stood in the doorway of Room 211 and shot himself in the temple with the Glock 19, dying just as police reached his position. Having prepared himself to do much carnage, police found 203 remaining rounds of ammunition in Norris Hall. All told, during the two attacks, Cho killed five faculty members and 27 students before killing himself. Additionally, 17 others were wounded as well as 6 who were injured in the jump from Professor Librescu's classroom.

Sadly, prior to the attack many saw things that appeared to be out of place. But no one did anything. For instance, before the attack commenced, a faculty member saw the chained doors. A note was attached that read a bomb would go off if the chains were removed. Contrary to protocol that police were to be contacted immediately, the faculty member carried the note to the dean's office. In another instance, a student heading for class found the entrance chained.

Assuming it had something to do with construction, she climbed through a window to get inside. Additionally, the university did not evacuate the campus or notify students of the first attack until several hours later.

There were also warning signs missed long before the attack. Consensus has it that Cho suffered from what is called "selective mutism." Cho had a history of mental illness and was known to be a loner. He was admitted to a psychiatric ward after telling his roommate he had suicidal thoughts. After a short period of inpatient care, he was released with orders to continue therapy as an outpatient. He did attend at least one counseling session at the Cook Counseling Center but then fell off the radar.

As further evidence demonstrates, unlike other mass shooters, Cho's motive and mentality were more readily apparent. For example, evidence found in his dorm room showed his actions were premeditated. In between the two sets of attacks, Cho had mailed a package to NBC News in New York. Received two days later, it contained videos and photographs of Cho posing with his guns, and a rambling document. In one video, he railed against rich "brats" and talked about being bullied and picked on saying "you caused me to do this."

Cho no doubt had delusions of grandeur, comparing himself to Christ, thinking of himself as some type of messianic avenger of the weak and

## Chapter 5: Awareness and Response in Schools

defenseless. Combined with the fact that he had purchased two handguns roughly a month before the shooting showed the attack was premediated.

The weapon's purchases proved in fact to be a single point failure. Cho had been involuntarily committed to a mental hospital. Federal law prohibits anyone from buying a gun who has been so committed. Thus, under federal law, Cho should have been disqualified from purchasing a gun. Falling off the radar, this went undocumented.

### Sandy Hook

Follow-on school shooters often emulated previous offenders. Adam Lanza, the perpetrator of the Sandy Hook massacre was fascinated with mass shootings, such as Columbine and Virginia Tech. In a copy-cat manner, on December 14, 2012, the twenty-year-old Lanza armed himself with an AR-15 and two pistols, entered Sandy Hook Elementary School in Newton, Connecticut, then proceeded to kill 26 people, 20 elementary students, ages 6 and 7, and 6 adults. Before this heinous attack, Lanza left his family home, brutally murdered his mother, Nancy Lanza, then proceeded to the school. The weapons he used were purchased by Mrs. Lanza and were kept in the home. He shot her four times with a .22-calibre rifle then demolished his computer's hard drive, destroying his premediated work.

At 9:30am, Lanza arrived at the school and shot through a window adjacent to a locked security door. The noise brought out the school's principal and school psychologist. Lanza killed them both immediately. The sounds of gunfire were accidentally broadcasted through the school's sound system. However, this served to alert other faculty. Then, in accordance with the established lockdown protocols, teachers immediately barricaded the doors of their classrooms with desks and chairs.

Being alerted to the shots fired, Teacher Kaitlin Roig immediately turned off the lights, and in under 60 seconds, she corralled her 15 first-graders into the class bathroom. Successfully keeping them all calm and quiet, Lanza apparently poked his head in the door of Roig's classroom, and finding it empty, moved on.[2] The shooter then made his way down to the classroom of teacher Lauren Rousseau. Forcing his way in, he then murdered Rousseau along with her fourteen young students, ages 6 to 7. He entered a second classroom, that of Victoria Soto. He murdered her along with six first-graders. It was about 9:35 am when the first emergency call from the school went out. Within four minutes police arrived and found the shooter dead from a self-inflicted gunshot wound. Police then secured the school and then evacuated students and faculty to a nearby fire station.

---

[2] Louis Klarevas, *Rampage Nation: Securing America from Mass Shootings* (New York: Prometheus, 2016), 21.

## Chapter 5: Awareness and Response in Schools

The fact that Lanza thoroughly planned his attack is underscored by the way he entered the school. Sandy Hook had earlier installed a new security system making it so every visitor had to be identified and buzzed in. Circumventing this, Lanza shot through the adjacent window. Arguably, a $25 piece of laminate film over the glass would have prevented that shooter from getting in.

### *Parkland*

On February 14, 2018, expelled 19-year-old student Nikolas Cruz exited an Uber at his destination, Marjory Stoneman Douglas High School. He wore a T-shirt with the school's logo over a bullet-proof vest, a backpack filled with magazines, and an AR-15. Arriving at 2:21 pm, Cruz walked through an open and unstaffed pedestrian gate. He then entered Building 12 through an unlocked door, and loaded his AR-15. One student encountered him just moments before the attack began. Cruz said, "You better go, this is going to get messy." Cruz then pulled the fire alarm sending students streaming out into the hallway and into the path of his bullets.[3] As gunfire erupted, students fled and hid in classrooms, bathrooms and closets at the sound of the gunfire.

---

[3] Sarah Lerner, *Parkland Speaks: Survivors from Marjory Stoneman Douglas Share Their Stories* (New York: Crown, 2019), 136.

## *Active Shooter Awareness and Response*

According to the school's "code red" protocol, teachers locked their doors. In the span of less than three minutes, Cruz made his way through the first three floors of the school, shooting through doors and windows. Cruz entered no classrooms and only shot those in his line of sight as they huddled in corners. Only those out of view were safe. Within the first two minutes, 23 people were shot or killed. With the death toll rising, Cruz repeated this action on other floors throughout the building, even shooting at fleeing students outside. All told, Cruz killed 17 people and injured 17 others before discarding his rifle and blending in with other fleeing students. He was apprehended some two miles away and surrendered to police. Though he has yet to be convicted, he faces the death penalty.

Looking back, warning signs were missed. Like other mass shooters, prior to the attack the perpetrator demonstrated several threat indicators. In the months leading up to the attack, Cruz made many threats. A full two years prior, a family friend reported an Instagram post by Cruz that stated, "I am going to get this gun when I turn 18 and shoot up the school." On YouTube he wrote "I'm going to be a professional school shooter." It is estimated that some 30 people had knowledge of Cruz's troubling behavior. Police records show that law enforcement was called to Cruz's family home 39 times. A former classmate described Cruz as troubled and said he

## Chapter 5: Awareness and Response in Schools

would set off the fire alarm, day after day, and finally got expelled in the eighth grade. Cruz was also known for threatening other students. After the attack, videos emerged in which Cruz recorded himself declaring his intentions to be "the next school shooter of 2018" with the aim of killing at least 20 people.

In the last analysis, Parkland was a security debacle. A public safety commission highlighted several failures such as unlocked doors allowing to access the school's campus. The school's staff had been warned regarding Cruz's expulsion and the fact he presented a threat to student safety. When a staff member saw him outside, he radioed a "code red" to initiate a lockdown of the school. However, there was no PA system. This could have been used to warn staff and students. This also added to the confusion as to the shooter's location.

Perhaps the most tragic aspect of all was the lack of action on the part of a Broward County deputy sheriff. He was assigned to protect students from such threats. Though he heard the shots being fired inside the building, he failed to take action and remained outside during the attack. He was arrested for his inaction and faces charges of neglect of a child, culpable negligence and perjury.

Sadly, in the wake of the attack, at least two students have committed suicide. See chapter ten for information on post incident treatment.

In light of such tragedies as Parkland, the obvious imperative is security and awareness. Pointedly, to make sure all the doors close properly and can be secured. Additionally, faculty need to be more aware of who's on campus, and be more aware of troubled students.

## ALICE system

It is an established fact that 70% of active shooter incidents are resolved before law enforcement arrive. In light of this, it's imperative for schools to be more proactive than reactive. The ALICE system promotes a "proactive" response to an active shooter incident that offers the best chance of survival. As formulated by Navigate 360, the ALICE system offers a purposeful response that consist of the following steps:

**A – Alert**. In the event of a potentially life-threatening situation, it is imperative to alert as many people as possible to the danger. Schools can use various methods, such as a PA system, email, or text. Due to the time sensitive nature of such attacks, a PA option would seem to be the best choice. The delivery of information regarding an incident will empower people to make an informed decision, maximizing their chances of survival.

## Chapter 5: Awareness and Response in Schools

**L – Lockdown.** Upon receipt of the alert, lockdown is initiated. To maximize the defensive nature of a classroom, teachers direct students to barricade the door. In the past, the best solution was to pile desks and tables in front of the door. Today, there are a lot of door barricading devices available on the market. If the door has a lock, lock it. If its equipped with a "self-closing" arm at the top of the door, secure the two arms together using a belt, or any binding material to make the door difficult to open. Once in lockdown posture, those inside should call 911 and prepare to defend against the shooter should he make entry.

**I – Inform.** As a continuation of alert, this step passes on real time information, communicating the location of the active shooter. The purpose of this step is to keep everyone informed in an effort to coordinate the best possible defense. Schools should have a PA system to rapidly disseminate information. Whatever system is used, updated information should be passed on, including when law enforcement has arrived, and when it's time to evacuate.

**C – Counter.** The aim of this step is to reduce the shooter's ability to dominate the room, thereby reducing the shooter's lethal potential. Physically confronting a mass shooter may not be the best option for everyone. However, if this is the last resort, then fighting for your life is the best option. Countering an attack can blunt or curtail deadly attacks.

Consider how wounded 17-year-old Jacob Ryker tackled Kip Kinkel, and held him down until police arrived, thus curtailing what could have been an even more deadly attack. Kinkel heard voices telling him to kill his mother and father and then attack Thurston High School (Springfield, Oregon). After murdering his parents, Kip arrived at his school armed with five firearms and over 1,100 rounds of ammunition. Before his shooting spree was brought to an end, Kip had killed 4 people (including his parents) and wounded 25. No doubt, had it not been for the aggressive actions of Jacob Ryker, the loss of life would have been exponentially more grievous. Kinkel is currently serving a 111-year sentence.

Besides swarming an attacker, others can make noise and movement to create a distraction to either enable opportunities to escape or eliminate the threat. For example, by his actions, Mandalay security guard Jesus Campos, distracted Paddock, giving people previous seconds to evacuate the field onto which he was shooting.

**E – Evacuate.** In this step, students are evacuated to a safe area, taking them out of harm's way. In the aftermath of the Parkland shooting, coordination was made to move the school's students to the convention

## Chapter 5: Awareness and Response in Schools

center at the Fort Lauderdale Marriott Coral Springs Hotel. This served as the Family Reunification Center (FRC), at which the American Red Cross and first responders set up water and snacks, along with mental health workers who offered psychological first aid.

### *Summary*

Since the 1999 Columbine massacre, there have been more than 240 mass shootings at schools, colleges and universities. Some 440 people were shot, 138 of whom were killed. In light of this, a few implications may be made. First, the selection of victims is still puzzling to law enforcement as no distinct pattern to their selection process of victims has yet to be determined.

Second, most attackers showed a prior history of gun use, and retrieved the weapon from a family member and from the home they lived in. Realizing when a weapon in one's house is missing or being used without permission might be an indicator that their family member is planning something.

Third, the motives behind school shootings are not the same as attacks in places of business or worship. It seems as though student school shooters attack their school, while shooters elsewhere generally have various other motivations, including hate and racism, as in the attacks on the Pulse nightclub, El Paso Walmart, the Tree of Life Synagogue, Fort Hood

Soldier Readiness Center, and the Wisconsin Sikh Temple.

Fourth, a few simple mechanisms can be used by teachers and cops to put time and distance between the killers and the kids. Lock the doors. Simply locking the door helps create a hard target. Have a single point of entry into every school.

Fifth, facilities should conduct active shooter drills within and in partnership with the schools in your city so teachers know how to respond, and know what it looks like when you do your response. Sixth, have an alert system that incorporates a PA system as well as email and text alerts, such as "Alert Us." Seventh, have a police officer on campus.

# 6

## Active Shooter Awareness and Response in Places of Worship

*"The prudent see danger and take refuge, but the simple keep going and suffer for it." – Proverbs 27:12*

In a 2009 briefing at the US State Department, Secretary of State Condoleezza Rice placed faith-based organizations in the world's top five "at risk" sectors and noted that places of worship are "behind the curve" compared to the secular world, in terms of safety and emergency preparedness. Since 1999, over 90 people have been killed on faith-based properties, all of which in active shooter incidents. Despite these numbers, many churches still do not make security a priority.

Being at risk, some of the deadliest mass shootings in US history have indeed occurred in places of worship.[1] As occurrences of mass shootings continue

---

[1] Consider the attacks at the following places of worship: 1999 Wedgewood Baptist Church in Fort Worth, Texas; 2001 Greater Oak Missionary Baptist Church in Hopkinsville, Kentucky; 2002 Our Lady of Peace Catholic Church in Lynbrook, New York; 2003 Turner Monumental AME Church in Kirkwood, Georgia; 2005 Living Church of God in Brookfield, Wisconsin; 2005 World Changers Church in College Park, Georgia; 2006 Zion Hope Missionary Baptist in Detroit, Michigan; 2006 Ministry of Jesus Christ Church in Baton Rouge, Louisiana; 2007 First Presbyterian Church in Moscow, Idaho; 2007 First Congregational Church in Neosho, Missouri; 2007 New Life Church in Colorado Springs, Colorado; 2008 First Baptist Church in Maryville, Illinois; 2009 Reformation Lutheran Church in Wichita,

to rise, those taking part in services in places of worship must maintain situational awareness. Moreover, it's the responsibility of leaders to develop and implement security/evacuation plans.

One of the traumatic aspects of mass shootings is they occur in places we all assume should be "safe." Everyone expects a combat zone to be dangerous but not a school, church or synagogue. Right?

### *First Baptist Church of Sutherland Springs*

It was a Sunday morning on November 5, 2017 when Stephen Willeford was woken from his sleep by his daughter Stephanie. Most Sunday mornings, Stephen attended morning service at his local church but this particular morning he decided to sleep in. His daughter immediately asked him if he had heard gunfire. A sound had stirred him from his sleep but he assumed someone was tapping at his window. As he got dressed, he realized it was the sound of gunfire. Jumping into action, Willeford grabbed an AR-15 from his safe. Without even taking the time to put his shoes on, Willeford ran out of his home towards First Baptist Church. Willeford recounts, "I kept hearing the shots, one after another, very rapid shots 'pop,

---

Kansas; 2012 World Changers Church in College Park, Georgia; 2012 Wisconsin Sikh Temple; 2015 Emanuel AME Church in Charleston, South Carolina; 2017 Burnette Chapel Church of Christ in Antioch, Tennessee; 2017 First Baptist Church in Sutherland Springs, Texas; 2017 St. Alphonsus Church in Fresno, Texas; 2018 Pittsburgh Synagogue.

## Chapter Six: Response in Places of Worship

pop, pop, pop,' and I knew every one of those shots represented someone, that it was aimed at someone, that they weren't just random shots."

A survivor of the shooting recounted his perspective from inside the church, "I thought it was firecrackers at first, and when those bullet holes started coming through the door, it was obvious it wasn't. Devin Patrick Kelley emerged from his SUV at around 11:20 a.m., armed with a Ruger AR-15 style-rifle, and wearing a ballistic vest, tactical gear and a black face-mask that featured a white skull. Approaching the church, he opened fire killing two people in the parking lot, then began firing through the door where worshipers were attending Sunday service. Once inside, he yelled "everybody dies, MFers." He then proceeded up and down the center aisle shooting people in the pews. Pausing only to reload, Kelley fired approximately 700 rounds in about 11 minutes.

As Willeford approached the old white church, he screamed as loud as he could, "Hey!" Those inside the church later recounted that when the gunman heard Willeford's cry, he stopped shooting and headed for the front door.[2] As Willeford entered the yard of a home facing the church entrance, Kelley emerged and fired three times in Willeford's direction. All three shots missed him. Willeford then propped his weapon

---

[2] Joe Holley, *Sutherland Springs: God, Guns, and Hope in a Texas Town* (New York: Hachette Books, 2018), 136.

on top of a nearby pickup truck's hood and fired twice into the man's chest. His first two shots hit their mark but were stopped by Kelley's body armor. Though he was not wounded, it was enough of a distraction to cause the shooter to stop firing and to hide behind a Ford Explorer parked in the church's parking lot.

Willeford took two more well-aimed shots, hitting Kelley twice, once in the torso and once in the leg. Kelley then fled the scene in a truck, and drove off at high speed. At that moment, Johnnie Langendorff, a friend of Willeford's who had witnessed the whole ordeal, happened to pull up in his car. Seconds later, Willeford and Langendorff sped off after Kelly, going at speeds in excess to 90 mph. Catching up to Kelly's car, Willeford called the police as they were in pursuit. They chased the shooter for around ten minutes, until Kelley collided with a stop sign, lost control of his vehicle, and landed in a ditch. Willeford jumped out of the car, propped his rifle on the hood, and demanded that Kelley exit the vehicle. Willeford saw no movement inside the vehicle but stood his ground. He recounted: "I never saw any movement, but I wasn't going to let him go anywhere." Police arrived at the scene around five minutes later. Upon inspecting the vehicle, they found Kelley, dead inside with a self-inflicted gunshot wound to the head. Asked what he was thinking at the time, Langendorff said, "Nothing. Get him. Because that's what you do, you chase a bad guy."

## Chapter Six: Response in Places of Worship

In the aftermath, death crossed three generations. Of the 26 deaths, one victim was 77. Another was 18 months old. Eight of those murdered were children. One victim was pregnant. Three married couples died together, as did a set of three young siblings. A total of 20 people were injured. How can such evil be explained? Stephen Willeford believes that what happened that day was a battle between good and evil. He says he was terrified, but he thinks the calm he experienced was the Holy Spirit taking over. He tells people he thinks it was the Lord's hand shielding him as the man doing evil fired over and over again in his direction. And looking back now, he feels as though God had been shaping him every day of his life into the perfect tool for that day. As Willeford said, "I'm no hero. I just wish I could have gotten there faster. God protected me and gave me the skills to do what needed to be done."

As in other senseless slaughters, things were missed. Kelley was court-martialed in 2012 on two charges of assaulting his spouse and their child. He was confined for a year at Holloman Air Force Base, New Mexico and was then discharged for bad conduct in 2014. Following his bad conduct discharge, Kelley made several failed attempts at obtaining firearms. However, due to a clerical error, he bought an AR-15 rifle. The Air Force acknowledged that an officer failed to enter Kelley's domestic violence court-martial into a national database which would have barred him from buying weapons. As to motive, it seems Kelley had targeted his mother-in-law, who was actually not present at the church that Sunday.

Many forget about security while they are in a place of worship. However, the days of worshipping without incident in America no longer exists. Proverbs 27:12 states that "The prudent see danger and take refuge, but the simple keep going and suffer for it." We must therefore stay in the yellow in today's society even while we are worshiping God. Demonstrating the perseverance of the saints, on the website of First Baptist Church of Sutherland Springs is the Scripture: "I have said these things to you, that in me you may have peace. In the world you will have tribulation. But take heart; I have overcome the world" (John 16:33). As we've seen, situational awareness (SA) involves detecting behavior threat indicators. There are certain patterns we may recognize that indicate an imminent threat.

The fact that churches are considered "soft targets" is evidenced from the long list of attacks. On many occasions, church leaders have been the target of the attack. For example, on the morning of June 10, 2002, Lloyd Robert Jeffress entered Conception Abbey, Kansas City, Missouri, and opened fire on the first person he saw, 64-year-old Brother Damian Larson, who died at the scene. Seconds later, Jeffress shot 68-year-old Reverend Kenneth Reichert, the prior of the monastery, in the abdomen, along with

## Chapter Six: Response in Places of Worship

73-year-old Reverend Norbert Schappler in the groin and leg. All told, Jeffress shot four monks, killing two and wounding two, before killing himself.

On October 5, 2003, 43-year-old Sheila Wilson had just walked into Turner Monumental AME Church, Atlanta when she shot and killed Rev. Johnny Clyde Reynolds after he greeted her and was walking away. Wilson then shot her mother Jennie Mae Robinson once in the head before turning the gun on herself.

On August 12, 2007, Eiken Elam Saimon entered the First Congregational Church in Neosho, Missouri. Armed with several pistols, Saimon had children and members of his family exit the building and then killed the pastor and two deacons, and wounded five others. Saimon was arrested after a standoff ended with police.

On other occasions, there doesn't seem to be any motive other than hatred. For example, just before 7pm on the evening of September 15, 1999, Larry Gene Ashbrook entered Wedgwood Baptist Church, Fort Worth, Texas. Opening fire, he killed seven and wounded seven others. From the time he entered the building, he fired over 100 rounds from two different handguns. He also threw a pipe bomb which fortunately exploded without hurting anyone. During the attack, Ashbrook yelled, "This religion is bull___", I can't believe you believe in this junk." He then sat down on a pew and killed himself. Investigators found no solid evidence for a motive other than the fact that Ashbrook hated God and the church.

## *New Life Church*

Two deadly church shootings over one weekend, in different cities, were committed by the same man. On December 9, 2007, 24-year-old Matthew Murray entered 14,000-member New Life Church to continue a murderous rampage that began at the Youth With a Mission Center (YWAM) the previous night. At 12:30 pm that Sunday morning, Murray arrived at the New Life Church parking lot, killing Tiffany Johnson and Phil Crouse. As Murray entered the church armed with an AR-15, he shot into the doors and hallways of the church, sending congregants to find shelter wherever they could. Murray was carrying an assault rifle, two handguns, smoke bombs and 1,000 rounds of ammunition. Sitting in a pew with others was Jeanne Assam, a former police officer. Armed with a concealed Beretta 9mm handgun, Assam was volunteering as a church security guard. Hearing the shots, she got up, and seeing Murray in the foyer, she recounts, "I stepped out and I said 'police officer, drop your weapon' and he turns around and pulls his AR-15 on me, and before he could pull the trigger, I fired the first five rounds very rapidly and knocked him back completely on his back." Assam adds, "I saw a sad, confused individual who forced me to end his life." Though Murray was injured and incapacitated

## Chapter Six: Response in Places of Worship

by Assam's return fire, the ordeal ended with the gunman taking his own life. Tragically two people were killed and three others were injured. Had it not been for the courage and quick thinking of Jeanne Assam, undoubtedly many others would have lost their lives.

In the aftermath, as police investigated the event further, it was apparent that Murray had a strong hatred for Christians and wrote numerous anti-Christian messages on various websites. In Murray's car, police found a letter which began: "To God: What have I done so wrong? What is wrong with me anyways? Am I really such a bad person? I didn't even ask to be born. Jesus, where are you? Do you even care these days?" The letter goes on to say: "The more I read your stupid book, the more I pray, the more I reach out to Christians for help, the more hurt and abused I get." Police learned that a shipment of rifle ammunition had arrived at the Murray household a week before the shooting.

In an interview, Assam credited her experience as a veteran police officer in providing the skills necessary to win a shoot-out with a heavily armed killer. "I have the training and I have the mindset. That's what all police officers need, you can't wait for SWAT." She went on to say, "These cowards are going to show up anywhere. They could show up at a restaurant where you're eating or at your school or at a concert venue.

So, I really want to emphasize that we need to be proactive rather than reactive."

An analysis of the above two shootings, as well as many others demonstrate how threat indicators often begin within the family and church community. This underscores the fact we must all be aware of signs of misbehavior, depression, hopelessness, inactivity, mood changes, anger issues, etc.

Many believe concerning yourself with church security is somehow a lack of faith. A fitting retort comes from Oliver Cromwell who in faith said "trust in the Lord and keep your powder dry." The fact that church shootings have become common place is underscored by the fact that there is now a church shooting database. In light of the attacks above, the days of being unaware of one's surroundings and unprepared are over. We must stay alert and prepared to defend ourselves, even at church.

### *Security Team*

Security is one of the hardest issues for a church because a church is God's house and should therefore be welcome to all. The challenge is to present a welcomed atmosphere with a potential to make a purposeful defense. Security team members should walk around the exterior of the building and check all exterior doors and windows. As part of an overall security plan, there should be as few entry/exit points

## Chapter Six: Response in Places of Worship

as possible. These should be manned with security personnel.

All other doors should be locked. Whether security personnel are armed or not is up to church leadership. If personnel are armed, they should fulfill all legal requirements and have sufficient training See chapter 9 for more on self-defense. Preferably, if security is armed, they should carry concealed. Optimally, those at security points should not only be armed but have two-way radios and access to a PA system.

Church actions during an active shooter incident should mirror that of schools. Using the ALICE system, an **alert** of the danger should be made using a PA system or other various methods. This will empower people to make an informed decision, maximizing their chances of survival. Upon receipt of the alert, a **lockdown** should get underway. For example, those in Children's Church and the nursery should barricade themselves in the room. As a continuation of alert, the church should be given real time **information**, such as location of the active shooter, or that law enforcement has arrived, etc. The purpose of this step is to keep everyone informed in an effort to coordinate the best possible defense.

Depending on where people are in reference to the shooter, the best option may be to take lethal action to **counter** the shooter. As noted, physically confronting a mass shooter may not be the best option for everyone. However, if this is the last resort, then fighting for your life is the best option. As we have seen, countering an attack can blunt or curtail deadly attacks. Lastly, at some point, congregants should be **evacuated** to a safe area, taking them out of harm's way. This reminds leaders to have an evacuation plan. Belongings should be left behind. This could be a fellowship hall or other identified building nearby. All this takes coordination. It is believed that these measures alone can mitigate a fair amount of threat.

As previously said, a church is God's house. It is supposed to be welcomed to all. The challenge then is to present a welcomed atmosphere as well as a purposeful response. While participating in worship, we may not always see abrupt warning signs. In other words, some attacks at places of worship aren't always so overt. In fact, the active shooter can actually take part in the service.

On Wednesday night, June 17, 2015, Dylann Roof entered Emanuel AME Church. He sat on a pew and listened to the whole Bible study, and as church members began holding hands in prayer, he took out his Glock 45 and commenced to shooting and killing as many as he could. It ended with 9 dead and one injured. As it turned out, Roof was a racist and enacted this horrible hate crime. Such evil is staggering. He later said, "I would like to make it crystal clear; I do not regret what I did." He went on to say, "I am not sorry. I have not shed a tear for the

## Chapter Six: Response in Places of Worship

innocent people I killed." One of Roof's motives was to start a race war.

Unable to find Roof on their own, the police released a photo and video screenshot of the surveillance footage taken of him inside of the church. Roof was on the run for 16 hours before his vehicle was pulled over in North Carolina. Police surrounded his vehicle and took him into custody. He is currently serving a life sentence.

### *The Sword and the Trowel*

As the reader may know, Nehemiah was a priest living among the captive Israelites in Persia and heard of the plight of Jerusalem, how its walls were broken down, and its gates are burned with fire (Nehemiah 1:3). Then, in his zeal for the Lord's people, Nehemiah returned to Jerusalem and set about to the task of rebuilding the walls of the city. Many leadership lessons can be gleaned from his approach to doing this. First and foremost, he acquired God's vision for the endeavor, that is, God put in his heart what he must do (Neh 2:11-12). Second, he was concerned with the safety of God's people, so that they would no longer be in "distress and reproach" (Nehemiah 1:3). Third, he set about to understand the situation before he offered any solutions. Fourth, he informed others only after he knew the size of the problem. Fifth, he cast a clear vision to the people. Sixth, he had good situational awareness of the people's enemies and would not allow himself or others to be discouraged by opposition (Neh 2:19-20). Seventh, he set reasonable goals and organized the people to work according to their gifts. And eighth, he positioned some of the people to serve as guards so that the others could focus on building the walls. Nehemiah 4:15-18 tells us how he went about doing this:

> 15 And it happened, when our enemies heard that it was known to us, and that God had brought their plot to nothing, that all of us returned to the wall, everyone to his work. 16 So it was, from that time on, that half of my servants worked at construction, while the other half held the spears, the shields, the bows, and wore armor; and the leaders were behind all the house of Judah. 17 Those who built on the wall, and those who carried burdens, loaded themselves so that with one hand they worked at construction, and with the other held a weapon. 18 Every one of the builders had his sword girded at his side as he built. And the one who sounded the trumpet was beside me.

Nehemiah's approach was the sword and the trowel. In response to the threat, Nehemiah prayerfully set up a guard force to enable the building of the wall of Jerusalem to continue opposed. It is hoped that the reader will readily apprehend the beauty and simplicity of this analogy and that the information in this book will arm you with tools to defend your flock.

## Chapter Six: Response in Places of Worship

### *Summary*

In light of senseless attacks at places of worship, a few implications may be made. First, most importantly, worshippers must get out of the mindset that places of worship are automatically "safe zones." This is not lack of faith. Consider again the allegory of the sword and the trowel. Second, leaders should organize a security team. The next chapter will discuss security teams in places of worship along with legal considerations. Third, like businesses and schools, places of worship need notification systems.

# 7

## *Self-Defense*

*"Since you don't know when something bad is going to happen, you have to be ready at all times in all places."* – Jack Wilson

Under US law, people are allowed to act in self-defense. That is, they may use force, including deadly force to protect themselves and other people. Stand Your Ground laws exist in at least 25 states, including North Carolina and Florida. Known as the "castle doctrine," this stipulates that someone attacked can use reasonable force, which can include deadly force, to protect his/her or another's life without any duty to retreat from the attacker.

The last chapter discussed church security, and amongst other things the challenge to present a welcomed atmosphere with a potential to make a purposeful defense. That certainly describes the actions of the West Freeway Church of Christ security team, of White Settlement, Texas.

Jack Wilson and other security team members, Tony Wallace and Richard White, had their eyes on the suspicious actions of a man taking part in worship that day. It was Sunday, December 29, 2019. The congregation had just begun to take communion as the security team made their way over to the man in question.

## Chapter Seven: Self-Defense

The man was 43-year-old Keith Thomas Kinnunen. Described by his ex-wife as "battling a demon," Kinnunen had a long criminal history. Arriving just before 11:00, Kinnunen was wearing a wig and a fake beard. Passing Kinnunen's behavior through the six domains of profiling (President George Bush knows his atmospherics), regarding *proxemics*, more than a few people felt uncomfortable and moved to another seat. Under the rubric of *geographics*, the perpetrator certainly looked out of place. This and his frequent trips to the bathroom alerted the security team. *Biometrically*, Kinnunen seemed nervous and fidgety. Regarding *kinesics*, the perpetrator seemed to telegraph his nefarious intentions, which was detected in others. The security team was newly assembled. In light of the recent shooting First Baptist Church Sutherland Springs, Texas, the congregation felt the need to be better prepared. However, the three-man security team, consisting of deacons, were very familiar with fire arms. *Heuristically*, the three-man security team had a sixth sense of where all this was going.

There were some 240 people inside the sanctuary as Kinnunen rose from his seat and briefly exchanged words with Wallace and White. The *atmospherics* suddenly changed in the room as Kinnunen produced a sawed-off shotgun from under his jacket, killing Wallace and White. Closing on the shooter, Wilson had to wait for people to get out of the line of fire, then with one shot, he killed the 43-year-old gunman and then kicked the shotgun away. The deadly encounter took only six seconds. Wilson took aim and shot the shooter in the head with a pistol from a distance of 50 feet. The whole thing was recorded on live-stream video from a camera during the church service.

If Wilson would not have been armed, and assuming police were minutes away, it's likely that several dozen people would have been murdered before police arrived.

Nearly a year later, on Monday, September 29, 2020, a grand jury declined to indict Wilson for the shooting. As explained by Prosecutor Tim Rodgers of the Tarrant County District Attorney's Office, the law allows bystanders to act with deadly force to protect others. Undoubtedly, the church security team's actions saved the lives of hundreds of people that day. Governor Greg Abbott awarded Wilson the Governor's Medal of Courage, saying "When faced with an evil that few of us will ever comprehend, Jack Wilson responded with strength, bravery, and with love for those in the church that day."

According to law, a person is justified in using reasonable physical force on another person to defend himself or a third person from what he reasonably believes to be the use or imminent use of physical force. The defender may use the degree of force he reasonably believes is necessary to defend himself or a third person. But deadly physical force

## Chapter Seven: Self-Defense

cannot be used unless the actor reasonably believes that the attacker is using or about to use deadly physical force or inflicting or about to inflict great bodily harm.[1]

Additionally, the use of force is limited to stopping a violent aggressor. What is often overlooked is an option of de-escalation. If the situation has not yet become deadly, and if the potential mass shooter can be dealt with without deadly force, then the encounter need not end violently. The situation and the response of the person will warrant your response. Force must be proportionate to the assault. However, deadly force should not be used to stop theft or damage to property. It should also be known that some states require a person to try to escape from an attacker before using force as self-defense. The imperative is to find out what your State requires.

In the State of North Carolina, there are several statutes you should be familiar with. N. C. G. S. § 14-51.3 stipulates:

Use of force in defense of person; relief from criminal or civil liability.

(a) A person is justified in using force, except deadly force, against another when and to the extent that the person reasonably believes that the conduct is

---

[1] Reinhart, C. (2007). Castle Doctrine and Self-defense. Connecticut General Assembly, Office of Legislative Research. See also Self-Defense Overview, 2016).

necessary to defend himself or herself or another against the other's imminent use of unlawful force. However, a person is justified in the use of deadly force and does not have a duty to retreat in any place he or she has the lawful right to be if either of the following applies:

(1) He or she reasonably believes that such force is necessary to prevent imminent death or great bodily harm to himself or herself or another.

(2) Under the circumstances permitted pursuant to G.S. 14-51.2.

(b) A person who uses force as permitted by this section is justified in using such force and is immune from civil or criminal liability for the use of such force, unless the person against whom force was used is a law enforcement officer or bail bondsman who was lawfully acting in the performance of his or her official duties and the officer or bail bondsman identified himself or herself in accordance with any applicable law or the person using force knew or reasonably should have known that the person was a law enforcement officer or bail bondsman in the lawful performance of his or her official duties. (2011-268, s. 1.)

There are times when deadly force may not be used. Such situations include stopping a simple assault. The attempted assault must be murderous or felonious in

## Chapter Seven: Self-Defense

nature. For example, violent language leads to violent actions, but violent language alone does not constitute an assault. The law requires there to be an imminent threat of death or great bodily harm. In this vein, trespassers may be in violation of the law but the law does not allow deadly force to be used to end the trespass.

Shortly after the shooting, Wilson told local news that members of his security team had conducted extensive training. "You prepare for the worst," he said, "and yesterday was the worst. I did what I had to do to save and protect the other members of the congregation."

Texas Governor Greg Abbott said, "I am grateful for the church members who acted quickly to take down the shooter and help prevent further loss of life."

### *Summary*

The law permits people to act in self-defense, using force, including deadly force to protect themselves and other people. There are times when deadly force may or not be used. This requires all of us to know the law.

# 8

## *Stop the Bleeding*

*"Trauma challenges an individual's view of the world as a just, safe and predictable place."* – American Psych. Assoc.

Unfortunately, even the best prepared and trained individuals can't always prevent injury or death. Sometimes innocent people, through no fault of their own, find themselves at the wrong place at the wrong time. In these situations, the goal is simple; don't become a victim and do your best to prevent or minimize death and injury to others. First, look around and gather any available first aid kit available. Do a quick inventory and see what you have at your disposal.

Since these active shooter/assailant events have much in common with the type of environment we expect in a combat zone, it's prudent to learn what the men and women in uniform are taught about treating casualties under fire.

In the military, Tactical Combat Casualty Care (TCCC) is provided during three phases: Care Under Fire (CUF), Tactical Field Care (TFC), and Tactical Evacuation Care (TacEVAC).

## Chapter Eight: Stop the Bleeding

### Care Under Fire (CUF)

The first phase, Care Under Fire (CUF) is medical attention provided by the combatant casualty or first responder to arrive at the scene of injury during an in-progress firefight. Typically, in a CUF situation, available medical equipment is limited to that carried by the casualty.

In the military, there's a saying: "The best medical care is fire superiority." This statement acknowledges the fact that team members cannot let themselves get distracted by a casualty, but rather must continue to focus on eliminating the threat(s) that will create even more casualties if not engaged within a timely manner. To the layman, the thought of letting the wounded lay unattended may seem cruel and callous, but in actuality this understanding is well thought out and is the best course of action for all involved. Let's examine in depth how the military trains casualty care during a firefight.

First, the military is comprised of warriors that are expected to stay in the fight if able, not automatically disengage when injured. If a warrior is wounded, he immediately moves to cover to prevent further injury, and performs self-aid until attended to by a first responder if needed. Once self-aid is performed, he gets back in the fight if able. If the warrior loses consciousness or, for whatever reason, is unable to get to cover and perform self-aid, then generally, other team members quickly assess if the casualty is in imminent danger of death or sustaining additional injury while they continue to engage the threat. If the incapacitated casualty is determined to be in immediate danger of death or sustaining additional injury (inside a burning building, massive hemorrhage, etc.) then a fellow team member quickly moves him to cover, delivers necessary aid using the casualty's supplies and then returns to the fight until the threat is eliminated or the casualty can be further treated without putting the team in danger or the mission in jeopardy.

To sum up the military's approach, the primary goal of CUF is to eliminate, remove or separate from that which threatens life. Some examples of things that threaten life are: An active shooter(s); a burning building; an uncontrolled external hemorrhage. Now is a good time to introduce the military acronym MARCH:

**M** – Massive Bleeding.
**A** – Airway.
**R** – Respiration.
**C** – Circulation.
**H** – Hypothermia.

The MARCH algorithm is synonymous with Tactical Combat Casualty Care (TCCC). It is a simple acronym for remembering the necessary steps in priority for saving lives in combat.

## Chapter Eight: Stop the Bleeding

The only treatment being performed during CUF is "M", which stands for massive bleeding. The injured combatant or first responder places the casualty's first aid dressing over the wound and possibly applies a tourniquet if needed. The "A" for airway management is generally best deferred until the later Tactical Field Care (TCF) phase. The reason is simple; airway obstructions during firefights in combat are extremely rare. An example of when one might be confronted with an airway obstruction in an active assailant scenario would be if an assailant was actually choking a victim. Nothing changes – eliminate the threat and the airway obstruction is resolved.

However, stopping life-threatening extremity hemorrhage is crucial. The number one cause of preventable battlefield deaths (approximately 60%) is hemorrhage from extremity wounds. In contrast, a loss of airway only accounts for approximately 7% of preventable deaths. This is why the military focuses on self-aid by applying a first aid dressing and a tourniquet if warranted. If a team member is worried about the unconscious warrior developing an airway obstruction caused by either the tongue or vomit, then the casualty can be rolled quickly onto his stomach during a firefight or placed on his side, the recovery position, if time allows during the CUF phase.

## Active Shooter Awareness and Response

Let's see what the CUF phase might look like in an active shooter scenario within a school environment where faculty have been properly trained and the student body thoroughly briefed on actions to take.

Imagine you are a high school teacher with a classroom full of students and you received a "code red". The school is in total lockdown. Your classroom door and windows are locked, the shades are all drawn and the lights are off. The paperwork with all pertinent classroom data has been posted and the children are all huddled under their desks being as quiet as possible. You've positioned yourself with whatever weapon you have at hand and are ready at any moment to defend yourself, but more importantly, to defend the children whose lives are in your care.

Suddenly, the door is kicked in and some children begin to scream. You recognize immediately that the perpetrator has a weapon and is a threat. He immediately fires in the direction of the screams. A student cries for help, yelling they've been hit. Needless to say, you're terrified, but your training dictates that you ignore the student's cry for help and attack the shooter. The shooter is caught off guard by your actions and as a result, you are able to wrestle away the gun. He immediately let's go of the weapon and flees when he hears the sound of officers quickly approaching down the hallway.

## Chapter Eight: Stop the Bleeding

Your actions saved several children from being injured and possibly killed. Yes, one child was badly hurt, but another student (the first responder) created an expedient dressing utilizing clothing and applied direct pressure ("M") to the wound thereby slowing the bleeding until paramedics arrived. In the CUF phase, the focus is eliminating the primary threat posed by the shooter while a student deals with the lesser threat of uncontrolled bleeding.

Before discussing first aid, it is important to remember traumatic events with casualties are chaotic, with lots of distractions and emotions running high. Therefore, prepare yourself mentally beforehand in order to be an effective first responder. Take a deep breath and do your best to remain calm; primarily for your decision making ability and so you present the casualty with the proper demeanor. Stay calm!

### Hemorrhage Control

Understanding the importance of hemorrhage control is critical to saving lives. Therefore, let's go over the most common item the military uses to stop bleeding and then what civilians might use as a readily available substitute.

The medical community's guidance concerning proper use of tourniquets has evolved considerably over the years. Within a relatively short period of time, tourniquets went from rudimentary contraptions comprised of rags and a stick, only recommended as a last resort, to today's state of the art, first line treatment for hemorrhage control (see figure 8-1).

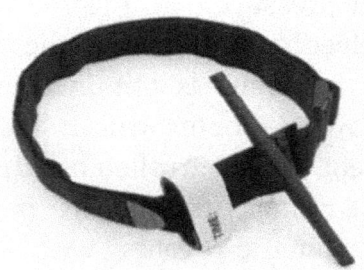

8-1 Tourniquet

The fact is, good scientific data doesn't lie. The medical community realizes the value of the tourniquet in reducing preventable battlefield deaths resulting from uncontrolled extremity hemorrhage. For the civilian, one can make a tourniquet from almost any available cloth-like material and something resembling a stick such as a good quality ink pen (see figure 8-2). Or for less than twenty dollars, one can easily buy a professional military grade tourniquet from any number of online retailers. They are small, compact and don't take up much space.

*Chapter Eight: Stop the Bleeding*

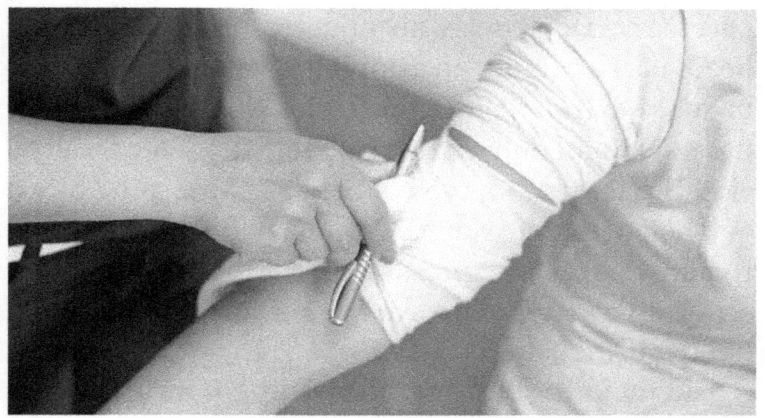

8-2 Hasty Tourniquet

Applying a tourniquet is quite simple. There are only a few things to remember. We'll use AARR:

**A** – Assess Injury.
**A** – Apply Tourniquet.
**R** – Reassess bleeding.
**R** – Reduce Complications.

We begin by assessing the injury. Approach the casualty with confidence and reassurance. Remain as calm as possible and get to work! Discover where the blood is coming from. This is crucially important. Do not be afraid to move the casualty in order to accurately determine where the blood is originating from. As we've addressed previously, uncontrolled bleeding is the number one cause of preventable death in trauma situations. Do not be afraid to remove, tear away or cut clothing to find the wound if necessary. Don't miss an injury on the back of the head, neck or under an armpit for example. However, in most extremity wounds, removing clothing isn't necessary and only wastes valuable time. A casualty's clothing serves as a type of bandage absorbing blood and helps clot the wound. Trauma to the head or torso requires applied pressure with some sort of absorptive material in order to slow or stop bleeding, not a tourniquet.

The majority of external bleeding injuries can be controlled by direct pressure. Therefore, when a wound is discovered, grab some absorptive material (perhaps your own shirt) and place it directly over the wound and apply significant pressure. Free flowing blood doesn't coagulate. Never remove old or existing bandage material: Just continue to add more material if necessary, in order to promote clotting.

After placing sufficient absorptive material over the wound and applying significant direct pressure, next elevate the wound if possible and let gravity help. Often the combination of pressure and reducing the pull of gravity on the flow of blood will be sufficient to stop or slow the bleeding and allow clot formation. If bleeding continues, then it's time to introduce the tourniquet.

Most likely, you won't have a well-designed medical tourniquet at your disposal. In the vast majority of emergency situations, you'll have to improvise. Choose material that is strong and pliable, but not too

## Chapter Eight: Stop the Bleeding

stretchy, and long enough to go around the limb with plenty of excess. If there is enough material to wrap around the injured limb numerous times, do so keeping the material as flat as possible. To minimize cutting, ideally the improvised tourniquet should be between one and three inches wide and have some padding underneath it to prevent skin damage. Readily available choices might be a necktie, bandana, leather belt, straps from a backpack or handbag, cotton shirt, or long stocking. Next, we will need some sort of strong, elongated stick or rod, at least four inches long, to use as a torsion device. Again, readily available choices might be small tree branches, a screwdriver or wrench, thin flashlight, thick marker, or strong ink pen.

Place the tourniquet "high and tight" approximately two to four inches proximal (closer to the heart) to the wound. Our goal is to cut off the strong blood flow within arteries leaving the heart before it reaches the open wound, thereby preventing blood loss. If we mistakenly place the tourniquet too close to or directly over the wound, the force of the upstream arteries will still leak blood into the wound. If the wound is just below a joint, such as the elbow or knee, place the tourniquet just above and as close to the joint as possible.

Once we have finished wrapping the injured limb with the tourniquet, we need to secure the wrap with a half-knot. Place the rigid object we're using as the torsion device directly over the half knot, then tie a full knot over it. Twist the elongated object until the tourniquet is tight around the injured limb and the bleeding stops. Secure the torsion device in place so the tourniquet stays tight and the knot doesn't unwind (see figure 8-3). Reassess bleeding to ensure the tourniquet is tight enough and bleeding has ceased.

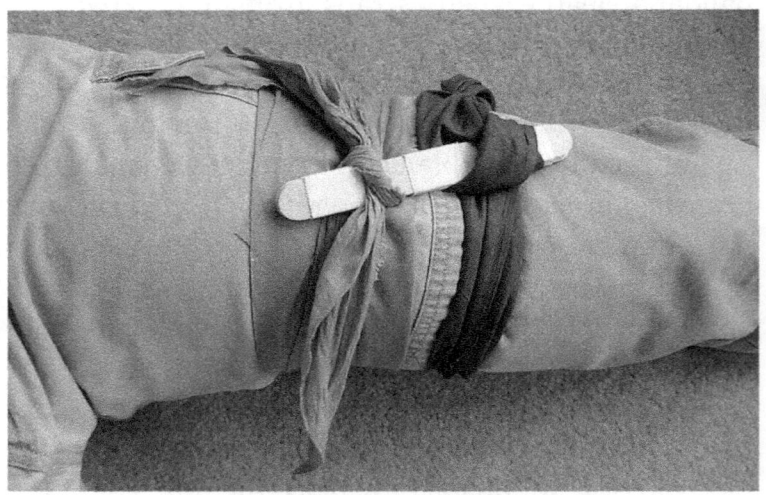

8-3 Expedient Torsion Device

Tourniquets are temporary solutions to blood loss, and therefore complications can arise if they are applied for too long. All people are physiologically different; therefore, research doesn't provide an exact time limit before the lack of blood supply starts negatively effecting tissue. As a general guideline, two hours is considered the length of time a tourniquet

## Chapter Eight: Stop the Bleeding

can be tied before neuromuscular injury (loss of normal function) begins and perhaps three to four hours before necrosis (tissue death) becomes a serious concern.

It is rare for EMS personnel to be delayed beyond two hours in active shooter scenarios. However, if you think medical help will take longer than two hours to get to you, then attempt to cool the limb down with ice or cold water, while elevated, in hopes of delaying tissue injury and loss of function. Mark the casualty somewhere conspicuous with a "T" to indicate a tourniquet has been applied and note the time it was applied. Lastly, keep the wound as clean as possible and make sure the casualty is kept warm and hydrated until paramedics arrive and take over the scene.

### Tactical Field Care (TFC)

The next phase of TCCC is Tactical Field Care (TFC). In military jargon, this phase of treatment begins when the good guys achieve fire superiority, and neither the casualty, nor the first responder is under threat of hostile fire. Typically, in an active shooter situation, this will mean either the threat has been eliminated altogether or the threat has moved along and is no longer in the casualty's immediate area. If the threat has moved on, attempt to secure your immediate area in order to prevent the threat from returning or, if feasible, move a short distance to a location that can be secured.

Once out of danger, return to the MARCH algorithm for treatment. You've previously addressed "M" for massive bleeding during the CUF phase. After quickly double-checking to ensure major bleeding has been controlled, proceed to "A" for airway and "R" for respirations. You need to make sure the casualty has a patent airway, meaning air can travel freely to and from the lungs and make sure the casualty is breathing. If the airway is obstructed due to severe facial trauma involving the mouth and nose area and the casualty is unable to breathe as a result, you may be forced to perform an emergency cricothyrotomy procedure with any sharp cutting object such as a pocket knife and use a small tube such as an ink pen with the components removed. Find the soft membrane located between the Thyroid and Cricoid cartilage and cut through the skin and then puncture the membrane with the shell of the ink pen (see figure 8-4). Check breathing through the tube.

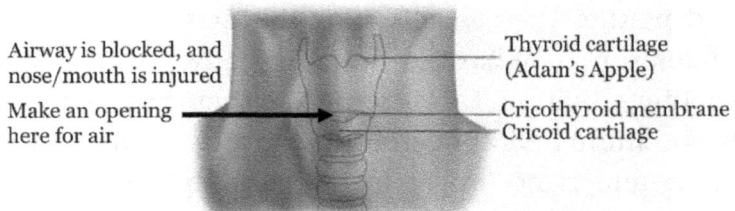

8-4 Cricothyrotomy Procedure

## Chapter Eight: Stop the Bleeding

In an unconscious, unresponsive casualty without facial trauma, we want to keep the casualty's tongue from blocking the airway. Check the mouth for any debris or foreign objects such as loose teeth, dentures, etc. Once the mouth has been cleared, a simple head tilt, chin lift or jaw thrust maneuver should open the airway and allow us to check breathing. Observe for chest movement, feel for breath on your cheek and listen for the sound of breathing (see figure 8-5).

8-5 Check Airway and Breathing

Thoroughly check the casualty for signs of trauma to the torso, front and back. Treat any puncture wound to the chest and back with an occlusive dressing (material that doesn't allow air to flow through it) to prevent air from being drawn into the lung cavity (see figure 8-6). Items such as a ziplock bag or a section cut from an unused plastic trash bag can be taped over the wound to occlude airflow.

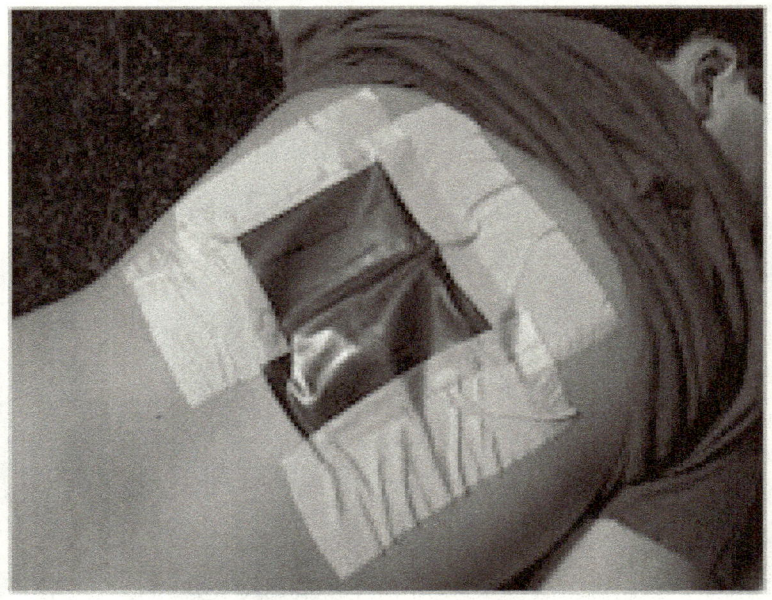

8-6 Occlusive Dressing

After bandaging any penetrating chest wounds with occlusive dressings, take your time to thoroughly assess breathing. If the casualty is having problems breathing, it is common for them to want to sit up rather than lay down on their back.

If you notice rapid deterioration of the casualty, severe respiratory distress, shock, and absent breath sounds on the injured side, you may be dealing with a life-threatening injury known as a tension

## Chapter Eight: Stop the Bleeding

pneumothorax. This condition is caused by trapped air that is being drawn into the injured lung cavity creating tension on the surrounding organs and blood vessels resulting in poor cardiac output, ineffective ventilation, and inadequate oxygenation. Treatment for a pneumothorax is decompression. Most likely, you will not have a chest decompression needle available to use, therefore attempt to let the air escape the cavity through the wound site currently occluded with the bandage. Lift up on the occlusive dressing and let air escape the lung cavity through the wound site. If the wound site has coagulated, you may have to reopen the wound using your finger in order to allow the air to escape. Find the hole by feeling with your finger until your finger is inside the chest cavity. Remove your finger and air should escape the chest cavity.

Once the chest is decompressed, you should notice immediate improvement in the casualty's breathing. Reseal the wound so air isn't drawn back into the cavity by the negative pressure created by the casualty's diaphragm. Repeat procedure as necessary.

If the casualty is unconscious and you're satisfied the airway is unobstructed and the casualty is breathing without difficulty, then place him on his injured side in the recovery position (see figure 8-7) to help maintain the open airway and allow you the ability to move on to other tasks.

After satisfied with the casualty's "A", airway and "R", respiration or breathing, we can move on to "C" for circulation and "H" for hypothermia. Do a thorough head to toe examination, looking for any minor bleeding and to ensure all major bleeding is still controlled by either a pressure dressing or a tourniquet. Address all minor venous bleeding with available bandage material.

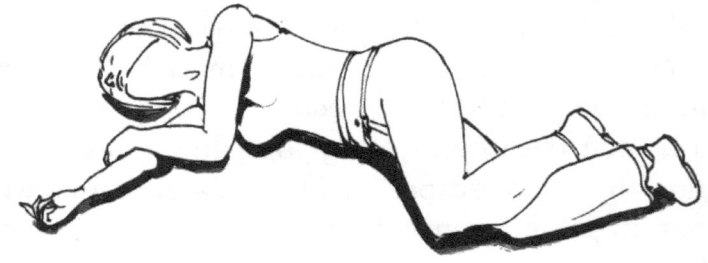

8-7 Recovery Position

Finally, keep the casualty warm. Remember that even though you might be sweating profusely and thinking about shedding clothing to cool off, the casualty is most likely struggling to maintain proper body temperature due to injury and inactivity. Use anything available to keep the casualty from getting too cold. Lastly, offer the casualty water if they are thirsty and reassure them that they will be fine and EMS is on its way.

The final phase of TCCC is Tactical Evacuation Care (TacEVAC). This entire phase will be handled by EMS once on the scene and encompasses the treatment the

## Chapter Eight: Stop the Bleeding

casualty will receive from paramedics during transport to the nearest medical facility.

### *Summary*

On October 27, 2018, the Tree of Life Synagogue of Pittsburgh, Pennsylvania was attacked by Robert Gregory Bowers. This hate-filled senseless crime claimed the lives of 11 innocent people and injured 6. Among the findings of an after-action review, two points stand out and bear relevance for this discussion: Acts of violence can happen anywhere, and the location of staged medical equipment matters.

# 9

## *Arrival of Law Enforcement & Emergency Medical Services*

"Courage is not the absence of fear but action in the face of fear."

On December 13, 2018, the mother of a 14-year-old called 911, alerting officials and potentially saving hundreds in the process. Brandon Clegg arrived at Dennis Intermediate School in Richmond, Indiana. He fired at a door to get inside the school. The school already was locked down after Clegg's mother called 911 to report a potential violent act. Clegg's mother reported that her son had taken her boyfriend hostage at gunpoint and threatened to shoot him if he didn't drive him to the school.

Once Clegg was inside, Principal Nicole Vandervort called 911 and used school security cameras to lead law enforcement to the armed teen. Then, after a short exchange of gunfire with police, the 14-year-old active shooter took his own life. No other students were injured in the incident. As the above example demonstrates, timely and accurate 911 calls save lives.

The following are some helpful tips to remember when calling 911. When they answer, the most important pieces of information they need to know is:

## Chapter Nine: Arrival of Law Enforcement & EMS

- Location of the active shooter(s).
- Number of shooter(s).
- Physical description of shooter(s).
- Number and type of weapons held by shooter(s).
- Number of potential victims at the location.

Additional information:

- Where you are: Office number, room, building.
- Hazards for those present and for responders.
- Other dangers in/around location.
- Safest approach.
- How many are injured?
- Types of injuries?

Remember that the phone lines may be flooded with a high call volume from people who may be trapped inside a building still. If you cannot get through to 911, that is a good sign that law enforcement is aware of the situation. When giving the information to the dispatchers avoid repeating yourself. If you cannot speak because it might reveal your location, keep the line to 911 open so that communications may be able to hear the events going on.

## Active Shooter Awareness and Response

### *Arrival of Law Enforcement*

While you are waiting for law enforcement to arrive, try to prevent others from entering an area where the active shooter may be. The average response time for police to high priority calls vary. Your actions during this first five to ten minutes is crucial. Moreover, the shooter may often not flee when police arrive. Remember, statistically, the goal of active shooters is to kill as many people as possible. When law enforcement officers arrive, everyone is a suspect.

On this note, if we are reacting to an incident, we need to be absolutely sure who the shooter is. Recalling the Gabby Giffords shooting, a guy mistook a hero for the shooter. Joe Zamudio was in a nearby drug store when the shooting began, and he was armed. He recounts: "I came out of that store, I clicked the safety off, and I was ready." As he rounded the corner, he saw a man holding a gun. "And that's who I at first thought was the shooter," he recalled. "I told him to 'Drop it, drop it!'" But the man with the gun wasn't the shooter. He had wrested the gun away from the shooter.

Likewise, as police enter the crisis site, everyone is a suspect and potential threat. Therefore, it's imperative you don't pose a threat to police. As law enforcement enter the building/area, keep your hands visible. Follow the instructions of any police

## Chapter Nine: Arrival of Law Enforcement & EMS

officers. Police will enter gun in hand. They will shout commands and may force people to the ground. Keep your arms up, hands spread. Don't run toward the police officers. Immediately drop any items you are carrying. Do not make sudden movements toward police. Do not impede the movement of law enforcement. Understand that the first wave of law enforcement will not help wounded people. Their mission is to neutralize the threat. A second wave of law enforcement will respond to the wounded. It's imperative to follow police instructions. If you are locked in a secure room, stay there.

### *Emergency Medical Services*

Officers attempting to apprehend/eliminate the shooter will not stop to help injured victims. Fire/EMS personnel will also be responding to the incident. However, entry by medics will be delayed until police are in control of the area and the shooter is eliminated or disarmed. As you provide first aid for a victim, be prepared to do trauma care until they enter. Additionally, do not attempt to move wounded people.

Once the incident has been deescalated, there will still be a lot of confusion. As response and recovery efforts are underway, phone lines will most likely be tided up. If you are outside the crisis area, remain there. Stay outside the perimeter and obey law enforcement orders.

## Active Shooter Awareness and Response

At some point, when directed by law enforcement, you will be able to enter the building to collect your belongings. By protocol, there will be an assembly area where everyone can check in and be accounted for. Remain there until you have been released.

### *Summary*

As has been said, when you are in any building, have a mental map. Know at least two exits you can run to, including windows that could be used. Identify places to hide. Identify potential weapons. Stay in the yellow and be aware of your surroundings. If you are using headphones or ear buds, have one ear open to outside noises to maintain situational awareness. When calling 911, give pertinent information. Keep the line open. Silence your phone. Once law enforcement arrives, do not look like a threat. Follow their instructions.

# 10

## *Post Incident*

*"Traumatized people chronically feel unsafe inside their bodies: The past is alive in the form of gnawing interior discomfort...The body keeps the score."* – Bessel van der Kolk

Mass shootings are over in minutes but the effect must be endured for life. Families grieve over lost loved ones. Communities are scarred. Intense feelings of grief, fear, and anger return as the anniversary of the event comes around. Survivors relive horrific scenes in dreams. As news breaks with yet another shooting, more grief and anger surfaces at the senseless, preventable violence.

In the wake of the Luby's Cafeteria shooting in Killen, Texas on Oct. 16, 1991, a number of support services consisting of volunteer mental health professionals were provided for the survivors. These volunteers sought to help counsel and bring solace to some 175 survivors, including those who witnessed George Hennard murder 23 people and seriously wounded 27 others. Several public buildings and businesses were used to provide help immediately after the disaster as well as longer-term counseling.

As noted, since 1966, there have been 160 mass shootings which have claimed the lives of over 1,000 innocent people. These figures, however, do not account for the untold number of people who have been physically injured in the attacks or exposed to such attacks. Their lives were all impacted in various ways.

When mass shootings occur, they psychologically affect people in a variety of ways. These include major depression, anxiety, mood disorders, and post-traumatic stress disorder (PTSD). In a post-incident survey, 136 survivors of the Luby Cafeteria Massacre participated. The survey was conducted by a team of psychiatrists consisting of Carol S. North, M.D., Elizabeth M. Smith, Ph.D., and Edward L. Spitznagel, Ph.D. According to their findings, following the disaster, 20% of men and 36% of women met criteria for PTSD.

The most widespread means of coping with the disaster after it was over was turning to relatives or friends (88%), and the next most frequent means was talking to a physician or counselor (50%). Fewer subjects coped by drinking alcohol (15%) or by taking medication (27%). While everyone involved in a mass shooting, survivors, eye witness, friends and family of survivors, will undoubtedly experience some form of trauma, not everyone will develop symptoms of PTSD.

According to Matthew J. Friedman, "PTSD is a disorder in which a person experiences trauma-related symptoms or impairments in everyday functioning that lasts for at least a month and

## Chapter Ten: Post Incident

sometimes for life."[1] PTSD may occur in people who have "experienced, witnessed, or otherwise been confronted with an event or events that involved actual or threatened death, serious injury, or sexual violence."[2] Such events may include a natural disaster, a serious accident, a terrorist act, war/combat, or rape, including those who have been threatened with death, sexual violence or serious injury.

Regarding posttraumatic stress disorder (PTSD), the type of symptoms that will present varies from person to person and most likely is based on their personal history and the nature of the trauma they have experienced. People may experience PTSD symptoms within one month of a traumatic event. However, in a delayed onset, symptoms may not appear until years later. The trauma is stored. The body keeps the score. These symptoms cause significant problems with normal everyday life, impacting social relationships and work situations.

What does PTSD look like? There are essentially four recognized PTSD symptom clusters. These are (1) re-experiencing, (2) avoidance/numbing, (3) hyperarousal, and (4) negative thoughts or feelings. People can also experience multiple symptom clusters. Just which symptoms will present appears to

---

[1] Matthew J. Friedman, *Posttraumatic and Acute Stress Disorders* (New York: Springer, 2015), 15.
[2] David H. Barlow, *Clinical Handbook of Psychological Disorders: A Step-By-Step Treatment Manual* (New York: Guilford Press, 2014), 62.

vary by type of traumatic experience, with no simple straight correlation.[3] Those with re-experiencing symptoms experience flashbacks, nightmares, memories and other intrusive recollections. Re-experiencing symptoms make people feel as though they are reliving the event. "Individuals may feel that they are in danger in the immediate moment. They may panic and want to escape. They may become aggressive or assaultive in order to protect themselves from the reexperience of threat."[4] Such intrusive recollections make normal functioning difficult.

Those with avoidance symptoms may become numb to events, and at times completely avoid anything associated with the traumatic events. As with other clusters, those with avoiding/numbing symptoms may attempt to gain control over what is perceived to be out of control.

Hyperarousal causes a person to remain always on alert. Such hypervigilance may be seen as an attempt to avoid becoming a victim again, and steer clear of more trauma. Such a state of hyperarousal can drain a person biologically and psychologically "in which emotions are heightened and aroused, and even minor events may produce a state in which the heart

---

[3] Smith, H. L., Summers, B. J., Dillon, K. H., & Cougle, J. R. (2016). *Is worst-event trauma type related to PTSD symptom presentation and associated features?* Journal of Anxiety Disorders, 38, 55-61.

[4] Adam Cash, *Wiley Concise Guides to Mental Health: Posttraumatic Stress Disorder* (New York: John Wiley & Sons), 40).

## Chapter Ten: Post Incident

pounds rapidly, muscles are tense, and there is great overall agitation."[5]

Fourth, are those in the wake of trauma who experience negative thoughts or feelings. This may include irritable and angry feelings, a persistent negative mood, fear, sadness, as well as guilt, anxiety or shame. All of these symptoms can cause sleep difficulties, exaggerated responses, irritability, outbursts of anger, poor concentration.[6]

In the wake of a mass shooting, not all victims will follow the "same trajectories in regard to the onset and decrease in trauma symptomology."[7] Some reactions may be slow or delayed to come to fruition. No matter where you are in the recovery process, support groups for survivors are therefore invaluable. As Briere and Scott observe, such groups allow homicide survivors to "learn from the similar experiences of others."[8] Support groups further help survivors make sense of their loss and have their feelings validated by others who share them. This in turn helps to reinforce positive coping skills.[9]

---

[5] Matthew J. Friedman, *Posttraumatic and Acute Stress Disorders* (New York: Springer, 2015), 18.
[6] Adam Cash, 42.
[7] Bonanno, G. A., & Mancini, A. D. (2012). Beyond resilience and PTSD: Mapping the heterogeneity of responses to potential trauma. Psychological Trauma: Theory, Research, Practice, and Policy, 4 (1), 74–83.
[8] Briere, J., & Scott, C. (2006). Principles of trauma therapy: A guide to symptoms, evaluation, and treatment. Sage.
[9] Blakley, T. L., & Mehr, N. (2008). Common ground: The development of a support group for survivors of homicide loss in a rural community. Social Work with Groups, 31(3–4), 239–254.

As Blakley and Mehr observe, "in moments of 'me too' realization, the support group becomes the epicenter from which the trauma shock waves are felt and safely stabilized"[10] Additionally, being a part of and participating in events within a community impacted by a shooting can promote well-being and recovery in the aftermath. All of which ultimately can have a positive and mutually beneficial effect on the overall recovery process.

## *Post Incident Services*

During the response to the 2016 attack on the Pulse nightclub, the Orlando Police Department assigned a designated mental health incident commander to coordinate the various services that were rendered. These included the monitoring of mental health care workers, the connection of families to available resources, ensuring a continuum of care. In an after-action review, regarding mental health care, several lessons learned were gleaned.[11]

(1) Develop a community mental health coordination and preparedness plan. This plan includes identifying a lead mental health organization responsible for the coordination and deployment. The plan should develop a centralized source of information including

---

[10] Ibid.
[11] Recovering and Moving Forward: Lessons Learned and Recommendations Following the Shooting at Marjory Stoneman Douglas High School, 2018.

## Chapter Ten: Post Incident

contact information, credentials, specialized trainings, and other applicable details. Because there were some well-meaning but underprepared people helping in the aftermath of the disaster, in some cases, more harm was done. And so, without correct training, "good-hearted volunteers can do harm." As also happened in Aurora cinema. Mental health service providers used in the post incident treatment should therefore have consistent training in specific trauma treatments.

(2) Mental health workers should be trained in psychological first aid to address the immediate needs of the individual and community. "Psychological First Aid is a supportive intervention for use in the immediate aftermath of disasters and terrorism."[12] It aims "to reduce distress, assist with current needs, and promote adaptive functioning, not elicit details of traumatic experiences and loses."[13]

(3) This plan should identify a mental health incident commander. The mental health incident commander should be a clinician or a government employee with the appropriate trauma counseling training or experience. This individual should be responsible to ensure: Screening of mental health and other

---

[12] Brymer, M., A. Jacobs, C. Layne, R. Pynoos, J. Ruzek, A. Steinberg, E. Vernberg, P. Watson. (2006). Psychological First Aid. Field Operations Guide, 2nd Edition. National Child Traumatic Stress Network and National Center for PTSD. Retrieved from
https://www.ptsd.va.gov/professional/treat/type/PFA/PFA_2ndEditionwithappendices.pdf
[13] Ibid.

caregivers to ensure that their skill sets are appropriate for individual and community-level care. Therefore, individuals should be connected with clergy and counselors who are vetted and properly trained, and particularly with mental health providers trained in trauma-specific, evidence-based therapies. Appropriate triage (initial evaluation) is completed and a treatment plan is developed and implemented by appropriate professionals for individuals – immediately following an event as well as over time. Coordination and implementation of the community resiliency plan.

(4) Mental health support is not a one-size-fits-all approach. Individuals should be able to receive referrals to mental health workers trained in cognitive behavioral therapy (CBT), trauma-focused cognitive behavioral therapy (TF-CBT), eye movement desensitization and reprocessing therapy (EMDR), or exposure-based therapies to address PTSD symptoms that may occur days and weeks after the incident; and be able to be referred to psychiatry for those with acute stress disorders, PTSD, or significant symptoms of distress. Alternative therapies may be offered after evidence-based treatments are explored.

(5) Particularly following a mass violence incident at a school or workplace, there should be services available in easily accessible, yet private, places. Ideally, options should be available both on- and off-

## Chapter Ten: Post Incident

campus so that people can choose where they feel most comfortable.

Mental health and other providers should avoid individual debriefings immediately following a traumatic event; ensure confidentiality; provide continuity of follow up with those who have sought services; and, identify those at risk due to direct trauma and exposure and follow-up with them specifically.

### *Summary*

There are normal reactions to stressful occurrences. However, a mass shooting is an experience much like combat. It's an "event beyond the normal range of human experience"[14] The National Center for PTSD estimates that 28 percent of people who have witnessed a mass shooting develop post-traumatic stress disorder (PTSD) and about a third develop acute stress disorder.

Moreover, it is estimated that those with PTSD are five times more likely to die from suicide. Recognizing PTSD, and other related trauma-related symptoms is therefore critical in the aftermath of a mass shooting. Survivors have to look out for each other. As in other things, prevention is the best cure. In the aftermath of a mass shooting, the overall goal

---

[14] Friedman, 17.

is to bring healing, to cope with loss, readjust to the new changes and to move on with life.

## 11

## *A Comprehensive Security PLAN*

*"If you fail to plan, you plan to fail."*

So far, we have covered quite a lot of material. At this point our goal is to put things together into a coherent and all-encompassing manner so as to arrive at a comprehensive security plan for your place of business, school or church. The following is offered as a means of tying things together into a physical security PLAN:

**P** – Preventative strategy (ALICE)
**L** – Layered security
**A** – Awareness training
**N** – Notification system

**Preventative strategy** – In the military, a security plan begins with a threat vulnerability assessment (TVA). Every facility faces a certain level of risk associated with various threats. A TVA evaluates the level of risk faced by any number of threats, including hurricanes, tornados, earthquakes, criminal activities, and mass shooters.

A TVA begins with threat assessment. Ask the questions: What is the neighborhood like? Does the neighborhood attract unsafe individuals? Who might want to target the building/facility? What is the likelihood of criminal activity in the area? What is the crime rate in the area? This may provide a good indicator of the type of criminal activity that may threaten the facility. It is also recommended to be in regular contact with the local law enforcement authorities to learn what criminal activity is happening in your area.

Having identified credible threats, a vulnerability assessment can be conducted. A vulnerability assessment considers the potential impact a successful attack can have on a facility. Like the threat assessment, a vulnerability assessment should include criteria that is identified and rated. The goal is to identify security gaps. Ask, how might a stranger see the security of your facility?

Another crucial aspect involves access control. Who are you allowing in your building? If your organization is the lone user of the building, how do contractors gain access? How are you conducting security screenings for new employees? What does the perimeter of the facility look like at night? Is it illuminated? Can your employees get to their vehicles without feeling apprehension when they walk from your building to the parking lot? Could they see danger at a distance? Does the facility have a perimeter fence?

Part of a comprehensive strategy is the ALICE system. As we've seen in chapter 5, the ALICE system

## Chapter Eleven: A Comprehensive Security PLAN

promotes a "proactive" response toward active shooter incidents, and consists of the five steps: Alert, Lockdown, Inform, Counter, and Evacuate. There are currently over 4,000 schools in America using this system.

**A – Alert.** In the event of a potentially life-threatening situation, it is imperative to alert as many people as possible to the danger.

**L – Lockdown.** Upon receipt of the alert, lockdown may be the best option. Once in lockdown posture, those inside should call 911 and prepare should the active shooter make entry.

**I – Inform.** As a continuation of alert, this step passes on real time information, communicating the location of the active shooter. The purpose of this step is to keep everyone informed in an effort to coordinate the best possible defense.

**C – Counter.** The aim of this step is to reduce the shooter's ability to dominate the room, thereby reducing the shooter's lethal potential. Physically confronting a mass shooter may not be the best option for everyone. However, if this is the last resort, then fighting for your life is the best option.

**E – Evacuate.** In this step, evacuation is made to a safe area, out of harm's way.

**Layered security** – There are three fundamental aspects of physical security: Mechanical, operational and structural security. As a first line of defense, mechanical security consists of electronic systems, such as security hardware including access control, monitoring systems, intrusion alarms, as well as CCTV, and door locks. These systems can only detect threats and breaches of security. What is needed to operate these are dedicated security staff personnel. Operational security therefore consists of staff and procedures. As a further tier, structural security are those architectural elements that offer natural surveillance and access control. All of these elements offer layered security.

To ensure the practical working of security, a security command center is needed. This is normally located in an area separate from the lobby. It's where a facility can be monitored and controlled. A question here would be, do the command center staff know what steps to take in an emergency? Do they know the emergency evacuation routes? Do they know where to have everyone evacuate the building?

**Awareness training** – At a minimum, awareness training should consist of the ABCs of SA, common threat indicators and the ALICE strategy. Active

## Chapter Eleven: A Comprehensive Security PLAN

shooter and awareness training should be conducted quarterly.

On May 18, 2018, ten people were fatally shot, and thirteen others were wounded when Dimitrios Pagourtzis, a 17-year-old student attacked his school. Despite the carnage of this heinous act of cowardice, Santa Fe High School, Santa Fe, Texas had taken part in active-shooter drills, which it is believed to have curtailed the attack's overall lethality. Acting on what they were taught, many students escaped death by finding cover and barricading themselves from the shooter. The shooter was engaged by police who had been stationed at the school. He surrendered after being shot. Pagourtzis faces a forty-year sentence.

**Notification system** – The average response time for emergency services in America is around ten minutes. Most critical events are over in less than four minutes. In light of these facts, it's imperative buildings, campuses, and churches notify others to the critical situation. Various methods are available, including texts, emails, PA, etc.

A critical question here is: Do you have a method of passing on this information? Do your new employees or students get some form of security and safety orientation? Do they know who to call in an emergency? Do they know the emergency evacuation routes, and do they know where they should meet after they evacuate the building so a headcount can be conducted? If we fail to plan, we plan to fail. In the event of evacuation, have you identified a family reunification center (FRC)?

## *Summary*

The philosophy of security we need to put ourselves on the best footing and ward off mass shootings is one that is proactive. Simple steps can "harden" a facility and school. Simply locking doors, posting staff at entry/exit points and remaining in the yellow will save lives.

# 12

## *Conclusion*

*"Facts don't care about your feelings."* – Ben Shapiro

Ultimately, there's no silver bullet option to the active shooter phenomenon. Such incidents are difficult to detect and are over in minutes. In nearly every discussion involving this topic, there are several key issues that always rise to the foreground: Guns, mental health, the media, the prevalence of violence in movies and video games, along with various other societal issues. All of these issues have been politicized in one way or another. In a random literature review of some twenty years, these key issues form the basis for every argument.

What is the root cause of the active shooter phenomenon? As we have seen, this is a complex issue but nonetheless it seems to be a socially engineered disaster containing several deadly ingredients. According to Louis Klarevas, there's a trinity of violence consisting of a perpetrator, a weapon, and a target. In other words, a deranged person, a readily accessible gun, and a soft target.[1] It stands to reason that these findings are accurate.

---

[1] Louis Klarevas, *Rampage Nation: Securing America from Mass Shootings* (New York: Prometheus, 2016), 29.

Following this analysis, the first ingredient in the active shooter phenomenon involves mental health. As discussed in chapter two, there is a prominent negative stigma associated with mental illness. However, while mental illness is a contributing factor, it cannot be deemed the root cause of mass shootings. We want to be careful not to perpetuate the myth that mental illness leads to gun violence, as has been erroneously stated by politicians and clergy, and everyone else in between.

For example, in a recent Pew research survey, despite a wide variance amongst Republicans and Democrats regarding gun laws, there was a bipartisan consensus of 89% Republican and 90% Democrat in favor of preventing the mentally ill from buying guns.[2] This reflects a misunderstanding on the part of many. Not all mental illnesses are created equal. They differ in degree as well as in kind, ranging from schizophrenia to gambling addiction. The point is, just because a person has a mental illness does not mean they are by default a danger to themselves or others.

Our laws reflect this balance. Under Federal law, 18 U.S.C. § 922(d), it is unlawful for any person to sell or otherwise dispose of any firearm or ammunition to any person knowing or having reasonable cause to believe that such person "has been adjudicated as a

---

[2] Pew Research Center, June 2017, "America's Complex Relationship with Guns."

## Conclusion

mental defective or has been committed to any mental institution." The argument that mental illness leads to gun violence is as prejudicially disconcerting as it is inaccurate.

Secondly, by far one of the biggest arguments in this debate pertains to gun laws. Many advocate that guns are the problem. In a radical way to control gun violence, many are calling for the repeal of the Second Amendment. At the center of the debate is whether people should be allowed to have semi-automatic rifles. The argument is it's the preferred weapon of choice.

However, the vast majority of mass shootings involve not assault-style rifles like the AR-15 but rather handguns. According to the Mother Jones database of mass shootings, from 1982 to 2018, 62% of the total 142 shootings were committed with handguns while 25% were with semi-automatic rifles. The remaining 13% involved shotguns.[3] Handguns are the most common weapon type used in mass shootings in the United States. However, semi-automatic rifles were the weapon of choice in four of the five deadliest mass shootings. Virginia Tech, the third most deadly, falls into the handgun category. But can it honestly be said that the AR-15 is the root cause?

---

[3] Jaclyn Schildkraut H. Jaymi Elsass, *Mass Shootings: Media, Myths, and Realities: Media, Myths, and Realities* (Santa Barbara: Praeger, 2016).

## Active Shooter Awareness and Response

The deadliest attack ever to occur in an American school involved explosive. On May 18, 1927, 55-year-old Andrew Kehoe, killed 44 (38 were children) and injured 58 others at his farm and the Bath Consolidated School, where he worked on the school board as treasurer. Kehoe left a stenciled message found on his fence which read, "Criminals aren't born, they're made."

Other arguments include red flag laws, bans on bump stocks, reduced capacity magazines, better screening for mental illness, more thorough background checks, and longer waiting periods.

Tellingly, a Secret Service 2004 study revealed that "only a safe school climate" has a chance of stopping shootings. The study identified 10 key findings.

(1) Incidents of targeted violence at school rarely are sudden, impulsive acts.

(2) Prior to most incidents, other people knew about the attacker's idea and/or plan to attack.

(3) Most attackers did not threaten their targets directly prior to advancing the attack.

(4) There is no accurate or useful profile of students who engaged in targeted school violence.

(5) Most attackers engaged in some behavior prior to the incident that caused others concern or indicated a need for help.

(6) Most attackers had difficulty coping with significant losses or personal failures. Moreover, many had considered or attempted suicide.

## Conclusion

(7) Many attackers felt bullied, persecuted, or injured by others prior to the attack.
(8) Most attackers had access to and had used weapons prior to the attack.
(9) In many cases, other students were involved in some capacity.
(10) Despite prompt law enforcement responses, most shooting incidents were stopped by means other than law enforcement intervention.[4]

To counteract the active shooter phenomenon, technical solutions have been forwarded with varying levels of success. These include: Metal detectors, using one entrance, and mandating the use of clear backpacks. While these technical measures can be very effective when used in conjunction with resource officers and law enforcement, it seems getting to the root of the problem requires a social solution.

In this vein, in the aftermath of Columbine, Stanford University psychologist Elliot Aronson, Ph.D., offered a solution in his book *Nobody Left to Hate: Teaching Compassion After Columbine*. Aronson's basic argument reflects the experience of the author as well as the prevailing theory at the time regarding the active shooter phenomenon. As a social psychologist, Aronson holds that school shootings cannot be explained away as the acts of deranged

---

[4] Bryan Vossekuil, The Final Report and Findings of the Safe School Initiative: Implications for The Prevention of School Attacks in The United States (Diane Publishing).

lunatics. Rather, he suggests that the principal problem is the social environment that characterizes most high schools, where bullying, humiliation, threats, physical abuse and social isolation are prominent.[5] According to Aronson, the shooters are usually those who are tormented by their peers. While he does not suggest that being bullied justifies murder, he strongly believes that the hostile atmosphere of most high schools is a major root cause of school shootings.

Echoing this sentiment, Dr. Julian Peterson observes that some 91% of school shooters were current or former students of the schools they attacked. Further, 87% were in a crisis at the time, 80% were suicidal prior to the attack, and 78% leaked their plans to others prior to the attack.[6] In a point that is well grounded, Dr. Peterson rightly argues that as a society, we have allowed this phenomenon to go on by turning a blind eye to those in crisis. In the vast majority of school shootings, the perpetrators attacked the school itself in a murder-suicide.

Eric Harris wrote he dreamed of going on a shooting spree with Klebold. Dylan Klebold wrote, "We've always dreamed of doing this, this is payback. We've dreamed of doing this for years. This is for all

---

[5] Elliot Aronson, *Nobody Left to Hate* (New York: Macmillan, 2001), 86.
[6] Jillian Peterson, Hamline University – Mass Shooter Database available from https://academicminute.org/2019/09/jillian-peterson-hamline-university-mass-shooter-database/

## Conclusion

the sh*t you put us through. This is what you deserve."[7] It stands to reason that preventative measures such as observant students and staff can reduce mass shootings. This calls for identifying students in crisis and caring enough to intervene. It stands to reason that this applies to businesses and places of worship.

Another critical aspect of this social solution is related to the fact that mass shooters want to be famous and the media continues to give them notoriety. As Tom Teves argues the single most motivating factor is a desire for notoriety. "The quest for notoriety and infamy is a well-known motivating factor in rampage mass killings and violent copycat crimes. In an effort to reduce future tragedies, we challenge the media – calling for responsible media coverage for the sake of public safety when reporting on individuals who commit or attempt acts of rampage mass violence thereby depriving violent likeminded individuals the media celebrity and media spotlight they so crave.[8] Violence begats violence. As Tom Teves rightly argues, the responsibility and power to reduce mass shooting resides with all of us.

In light of this, it stands to reason that a social condition lies at the root of the problem.

---

[7] Ralph W. Larkin, *Comprehending Columbine* (Philadelphia: Temple Press, 6.
[8] Tom Teves, No Notoriety, available from: https://nonotoriety.com/

While it's beyond the scope of this book to give full treatment to all of these issues, one thing is for certain, as a Nation, while we work to find a solution, it stands to reason we need to be more diligent to keep guns out of the hands of the wrong people. One of the slogans of the National Rifle Association (NRA) is "to stop a bad guy with a gun it takes a good guy with a gun." Though this is often lampooned, it is nonetheless true.

Currently most schools ban firearms, not only on the premises, but also in the surrounding areas (including parking lots and adjacent properties). In light of this known fact, cowards with guns kill innocent people. They love target rich environments. Schools, churches, and most businesses are understood to be "gun free zones." Shooters bet on the fact that these targets are soft. It stands to reason then, just as mass shooters are deterred by the presence of police and armed security at schools, they would be deterred by the possibility of law-abiding citizens carrying guns. As argued by John Lott, "At least permitting school employees access to guns would seem to make schools less vulnerable to mass shootings."[9]

However, many do not agree with this logic, arguing that the presence of armed security and police in schools traumatizes students. Amid calls for

---

[9] John R. Lott, *More Guns, Less Crime: Understanding Crime and Gun Control Laws* (Chicago: University of Chicago Press, 2013), 118.

## Conclusion

defunding police and citing "traumatic presence," some educational officials are cancelling their long-standing contracts with law enforcement who provide security in schools.

Accordingly, school boards in Seattle, Oakland, Denver, and Milwaukee have voted to end mutual aid agreements with local law enforcement agencies that provided work for police officers on campuses. The rational? The presence of armed security officers on school premises "prohibits" many students from feeling safe and welcome. It complicates the obvious to say that one of the major deterrents in school violence has been the presence of school resource officers. It seems these educators are gambling with the lives of students in order to earn political points.

Over against the position of removing "traumatic presence," among the recommendation of the Final Report of the Federal Commission on School Safety was "Those best positioned to respond to acts of violence are those with specialized training such as school resource officers (SROs) who are generally sworn law enforcement officers."[10] Moreover, according to findings, "total casualties could have been higher in Parkland, Florida, had the school not provided active shooter preparedness training to staff (the latest training coming just six weeks before the shooting incident)." Finally, a key recommendation of

---

[10] Final Report of the Federal Commission on School Safety. Presented to the President of the United States, 14.

the commission found that, "States should consider requiring or providing funding for all school districts and individual schools to develop and (on no less than an annual basis) provide training and exercises on comprehensive active shooter preparedness programs."[11]

In summary, it may be safely said that the root of the active shooter phenomenon is not mental illness or even guns, rather it's a fatal coalescence of a deranged person, a readily accessible gun, and a soft target.

Ultimately, and you saw this coming, there isn't a silver bullet approach to this problem. There's no ultimate preventative measure to stopping an active shooter incident from happening. To argue one is unrealistic. However, by working together, law-abiding citizens, together with law enforcement, can establish doable strategies to make where we live and work harder targets. We can develop doable security and response plans that will put our best foot forward and lessen the potential for such senseless acts of cowardly evil to be perpetrated against those we love and seek to protect.

Inherent to this phenomenon is its unpredictable nature. In the last analysis, because active shooter situations are often over within 4-5 minutes, often before law enforcement has enough time to react, individuals have to be prepared mentally and

---

[11] Ibid., 151.

## Conclusion

physically to deal with the deadly encounter. Prevention is therefore the best cure. When out of our homes, we have to stay in the yellow, read the human terrain and be ready to fight for your life.

On April 30, 2019, on the last day of classes for the Spring semester at UNC Charlotte, former student Trystan Andrew Terrell burst into Room 236 in the Kennedy Building. There were some 60 students present. Upon opening the door, Terrell smiled and opened fire. The classroom emptied in panic, some barricaded themselves in nearby offices and called 911. As Terrell continued firing his handgun, student Riley Howell tackled him, knocking him to the floor, yelling "go, go, go!" to his fellow classmates. As Howell tackled the shooter, he was shot at least three times. While Howell's actions saved other students, giving them time to escape, it cost him his life. One other student died and four were injured. The gunman later recounted that Howell's actions had caused him to stop firing.

Riley Howell had no option of "run or hide," so he fought. The significance of Howell's action should not be downplayed. In the face of evil, he thought of others more than himself, and traded his future for the lives of others. "Greater love has no one than this, than to lay down one's life for his friends" (John 15:13).

Importantly, active shooter drills should be trained on a larger scale, involving police and first responders. This type of training creates shared understanding of everyone's roles and responsibilities, and gives everyone an experiential template to draw from. In training, gaps are identified which in turn could be determining factors in saving lives. It stands to reason then that prevention is the best cure. While we are seeking to find the best solution to mass shootings, let's keep our children protected.

John Stuart Mill once observed, "Bad men need nothing more to compass their ends then that good men should look on and do nothing."

Above all, in this fight against senseless violence, mental preparation is paramount. As has been said, the mind is the first and most influential weapon that we can employ into any dangerous encounter. When you have prepared and you're aware, you'll be able to think your way out of a thousand more situations than you will ever fight your way out of.

# About the Author

Paul D. LeFavor retired from the US Army Special Forces in 2009 after twenty years of exemplary service. Paul had the distinct honor and privilege to serve with some of America's best units to include the 1st, 3rd, 5th and 10th Special Forces Groups and Special Forces Operational Detachment - Delta. His civilian education includes a B.S. from Liberty University, a M.A. in Religion from Reformed Theological Seminary and a M.Div. from Liberty Theological Seminary. Among his many activities, Paul teaches leadership and unconventional warfare at the John F. Kennedy Special Warfare Center and School. His books include the *US Army Small Unit Tactics Handbook* (2013), *Iron Sharpening Iron* (2015), *Unto the Thousandth Generation* (2017), *Tactical Leadership* (2019), and *God's Man* (2020).

# Annex A

# Fundamentals of Marksmanship

*"When the crap hits the fan you won't rise to the occasion, you'll default to your level of training."* – Barrett Tillman

In this portion of the book, the goal is to familiarize you with the basics of marksmanship. With such a foundation laid, our chances of survival in an active shooter situation increases exponentially. In this chapter we will discuss the following:

1. Cardinal Rules of Weapon Safety.
2. Fundamentals of Marksmanship.

### Cardinal Rules of Weapon Safety

1. Always treat every weapon as if it's loaded.
2. Don't point your weapon at anything you're not willing to destroy.
3. Keep your finger off the trigger until you are ready to engage.
4. Always be sure of your target, and what is behind and in front of it.

## The Fundamentals of Marksmanship

There are tried and true fundamentals of marksmanship, which when properly understood and used, enable us to surgically apply accurate fire to all situations. Whenever a situation warrants the application of deadly force, we must be able to deliver well-aimed shots to eliminate the threat. Being proficient in the following marksmanship fundamentals will enable us to handle active shooter challenges without causing unnecessary collateral damage.

## Fundamentals of Pistol Marksmanship

1. *Stance*: The feet should be shoulder width apart. The non-firing foot is slightly forward of the firing foot (2 to 4 inches) and is pointed to provide you with balance. Use your back foot (firing foot) to quickly generate either forward or lateral movement. Your knees will be slightly bent and your upper torso leaning forward. You should have 60-70 percent of your weight forward to absorb the recoil of the weapon. The elbows should be locked into the body. Stand with your shoulders and head square to the target and your head erect. Key Point: Your stance should be athletic and aggressive.

2. *Grip*: Begin the proper grip by holding the pistol with a firm handshake type of grip with your firing

## Annex A: Fundamentals of Marksmanship

hand. The support hand is then wrapped around the firing hand, apply a clamshell grip by making a fist over your firing hand. The thumb of your support hand should be over the thumb of the firing hand, and the index finger of the weak hand should be under the trigger guard. Key point: Firing hand grip firm handshake (30%), support hand clamshell grip (70%).

*3. Presentation:* This brings the pistol up to your sight line (sight line is when your sights and target are aligned). Push the pistol out to full presentation while taking the slack out of the trigger.

*4. Sight Alignment:* Is accomplished by centering the front sight blade with the rear sight notch. The top of the front sight must be level with the top of the rear sight and in alignment with the eye (If you are not sure which is your dominant eye, there is a simple test. Extend your arm and point your finger at an object. Close your left eye and close your right eye and again observe your finger. Whichever eye observes the finger pointing directly at the object is your dominant eye).

*5. Sight Picture*: Is the positioning of the weapon's sights in relation to the target as seen by the shooter when he aims the weapon. A correct sight picture consists of proper sight alignment with the front sight placed center mass of the target. The eye can focus on only one object at a time at different distances. Therefore, the last focus of the eye is always on the front sight. When the front sight is seen clearly, the rear sight and target will be out of focus.

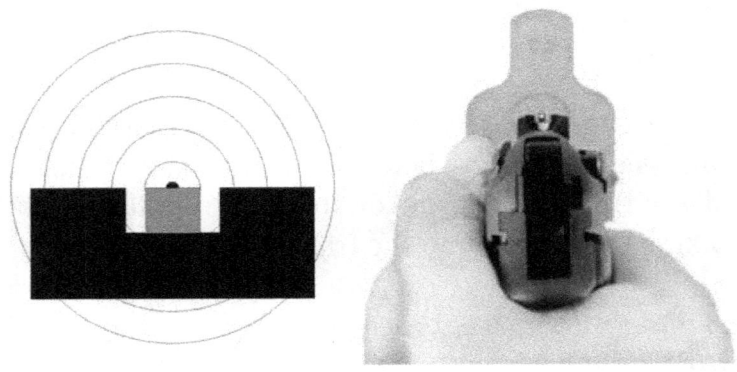

Proper Sight Picture/Sight Alignment.

6. *Trigger Control:* Apply positive increase of pressure smoothly and evenly to the rear without interruption as you're raising the weapon to the target, acquire a sight picture, continue to apply positive, smooth pressure to the rear, and fire. Single-action is between 4.0 and 6.5 pounds. When fired in the double-action mode, it is between 9.5 and 16.5 pounds.

After the completion of the trigger pull, release the trigger without losing contact between the trigger

## Annex A: Fundamentals of Marksmanship

finger and the trigger and remove the slack to prepare to fire again.

*7. Follow Through:* Is the conscious effort to maintain concentration on sight alignment after the shot breaks, and taking your second sight picture after the shot.

*8. Recovery:* Is the return of the weapon to full presentation and a natural alignment of the sights. If you use the proper stance and the correct grip and arm position, the recovery is more natural and uniform. Recovery resumes the sequence of applying the fundamentals for the next shot.

### Fundamentals of Rifle Marksmanship

*1. Steady position:* The rifle hand guard rests on the heel of the hand in the "v" formed by the thumb and fingers. The grip of the non-firing hand is light, and slight rearward pressure is applied. The butt of the stock is placed in the pocket of the firing shoulder. This reduces the effect of the recoil and helps ensure a steady position. The firing hand grasps the pistol grip so that it fits the "v" formed by the thumb and forefinger.

The forefinger is placed on the trigger so that the lay of the rifle is not disturbed when the trigger is squeezed. A slight rearward pressure is applied by the remaining three fingers to ensure that the butt of the stock remains in the pocket of the shoulder, thus minimizing the effect of the recoil. Firing elbow placement: The location of the firing elbow is important in providing balance. The exact location, however, depends on the firing/fighting position used for example, kneeling, prone, or standing. Placement should allow shoulders to remain level.

The non-firing elbow is positioned firmly under the rifle to allow for a comfortable and stable position. When you engage a wide sector of fire, moving targets, and targets at various elevations, your non-firing elbow should remain free from support.

Stock weld: The stock weld is taught as an integral part of various positions. Two key factors emphasized are that the stock weld should provide for a natural line of sight through the center of the rear sight aperture to the front sight post and to the target. The firer's neck should be relaxed, allowing his cheek to fall naturally onto the stock. This provides consistency in aiming, which is the purpose of obtaining a correct stock weld. Proper eye relief is obtained when you establish a good stock weld. There is normally a small change in eye relief each time you assumes a different firing position.

Natural point of aim: When you assume a firing position, orient your rifle in the general direction of the target. Then adjust your body to bring the rifle and sights exactly in line with the desired aiming point. When using proper support and consistent stock

## Annex A: Fundamentals of Marksmanship

weld, you should have your rifle and sights aligned naturally on the target. As the rifle fires, the muscles tend to relax, causing the front sight to move away from the target toward the natural point of aim. Adjusting this point to the desired point of aim eliminates this movement. When multiple target exposures are expected (or a sector of fire must be covered) adjust your natural point of aim to the center of the expected target exposure area (or center of sector).

*2. Aim:* Obtain sight picture and sight alignment as above.

*3. Breath Control:* There is a moment of natural respiratory pause while breathing when most of the air has been exhaled from the lungs and before inhaling. Breathing should stop after most of the air has been exhaled during the normal breathing cycle.

*4. Trigger squeeze:* Apply positive increase of pressure smoothly and evenly to the rear without interruption as you're raising the weapon to the target, acquire a sight picture, continue to apply positive, smooth pressure to the rear, and fire.

# *Index*

| | | | |
|---|---|---|---|
| Active shooter definition | 1 | Las Vegas Shooting | 61 |
| ALICE System | 74 | Librescu, L. | 66 |
| Assam, J. | 86 | Luby's Cafeteria | 59 |
| Atlanta Day Trade | 62 | MARCH | 102 |
| Aurora Shooting | 60 | Murder-suicide | 30, 142 |
| Behavior-profiling | 16 | New Life Church | 86 |
| Columbine | 8, 30 | No Notoriety | 143 |
| Common Threat Characteristics | 35 | NRA | 144 |
| Copycat Effect | 32 | OODA Loop | 22, 41 |
| Dayton Shooting | 9 | Post-Traumatic Stress Disorder | 123 |
| Detect-Deny-Defend | 46 | Pulse Nightclub | 54 |
| Emergency Medical Services | 121 | Riley Howell | 147 |
| Emmanuel AME | 90 | Run, Hide, Fight | 46 |
| Fight or Flight Response | 40 | Sandy Hook | 69 |
| Giffords, G. | 62 | Santa Fe Shooting | 138 |
| Grossman, D. | 32 | San Ysidro McDonalds | 59 |
| Hammond, K. | 60 | Second Amendment | x, 132 |
| Hupp, S. | 59 | | |

## *Active Shooter Awareness and Response*

| | |
|---|---|
| Situational Awareness | 7 |
| Societal Variables | 31 |
| Stoneman Douglas | 72 |
| Sutherland Springs | 81 |
| Sympathetic Nervous System | 36 |
| Thurston High School | 75 |
| Threat Vulnerability Assessment (TVA) | 131 |
| Tree of Life Synagogue | 77 |
| Trolley Square Mall | 60 |
| UNC Charlotte | 147 |
| Virginia Tech | 66 |
| West Freeway Church of Christ | 94 |
| Willeford, S. | 80 |
| Wilson, J. | 94 |

# Other Books by Blacksmith Publishing

Small Unit Tactics Handbook      Iron Sharpening Iron      Tactical Leadership

Marriage is a Four-Letter Word      Fire in the Jungle      Unto the Thousandth Generation

God's Man      # Fail      Confederate Black Ops

*www.blacksmithpublishing.com*

# Notes

www.ingramcontent.com/pod-product-compliance
Lightning Source LLC
Chambersburg PA
CBHW020255030426
42336CB00010B/779